Praise for *Love*

"A sweeping hero's journey into the mythic realms and magical healing of mushroom shamanism, Shonagh Home's *Love and Spirit Medicine* offers a potent message for the illumination of the human spirit and the awakening of the planetary heart."
—Talat Jonathan Phillips, author of *The Electric Jesus: The Healing Journey of a Contemporary Gnostic*, co-founder of Evolver

"In writing rich in heart, mind and intuition, Shonagh Home lets us accompany her through her life transformations via her relationships with both human teachers and plant teachers. Along the way, her narrative of crises endured and transcended describes her own inner spiritual growth and at the same time helps her readers grow in love and understanding."
—Thomas B. Roberts, Ph,D, author of *The Psychedelic Future of the Mind*

"In *Love and Spirit Medicine* Shonagh Home reminds us that our one true love, and our one true home, is always within ourselves. Through her honest and vivid ceremonial adventures with psychedelic mushroom spirits, Shonagh's heartaches become heart truths and life changing medicine. Home's mushroom memoir proudly walks along the newly growing path of psychedelic non-fiction favorites like *Singing to the Plants*, *Black Smoke*, and *Breaking Open the Head*."
—Adam Elenbaas, author of *Fishers of Men: The Gospel of an Ayahuasca Vision Quest* and one of the founding writers at *RealitySandwich.com*

"Shonagh Home's vivid encounters with spirit guides teach her about the shadow side of her psyche. She offers honest accounts of the confusions and misunderstandings that can occur during highly altered states of consciousness and the challenges of finding herself between the worlds. *Love and Spirit Medicine* is a courageous story of her shamanic initiation and her journey of awakening and empowerment."
—Annie Oak, journalist, filmmaker, and founder of *The Women's Visionary Congress*

"Shonagh Home does a remarkable job putting words to an experience that is almost impossible to describe. Her vulnerability and raw honesty is an inspiration and guidepost for all of us who are either on this journey or desiring to be."

—Kathleen Hosner, Ph.D.

"*Love and Spirit Medicine* is heartfelt and engaging, a fascinating story of one woman's shamanic path to liberation. It provides hard-won insight for others, particularly women searching for identity and healing, who would find themselves with spirit guides, on shamanic journeys, through the ingestion of sacred (psychoactive) mushrooms. Western doctors would do well to try to find commonalities with the shamanic approach Home uses, viewing shamanism and efforts such as Home's shamanic path as a source of convergent validity, not the rejected "other." Shonagh Home shares her personal journey from a dying marriage, through an array of fascinating shamans and other teachers, as a conduit for spirit, and ultimately to a place of self-knowledge and service. Written with humor and infinite heart, *Love and Spirit Medicine* is an immediate classic of transformative personal and spiritual development.

—Neal M. Goldsmith, Ph.D.
Public speaker and author of, *Psychedelic Healing: The Promise of Entheogens for Psychotherapy and Spiritual Development*
www.nealgoldsmith.com/psychedelics

"*Love and Spirit Medicine* is a poignant and brutally honest memoir about personal empowerment and transformation in a time of rapid global change. Full of humor and heartbreak, one woman's deeply personal journey toward self-discovery becomes a roadmap for individual and collective healing beyond cultural programming. Shonagh Home shows that by trusting inner wisdom and learning from one's shadow, one can see life's fiercest challenges as opportunities for conscious growth. It is a powerful testament for our evolutionary potential."

—Nese Devenot, Founder of the Psychedemia Conference and Contributing Editor for Reality Sandwich

Love and Spirit Medicine

· · · · · · ·

SHONAGH HOME

**TURNING
STONE
PRESS**

First published in 2013 by Turning Stone Press, an
imprint of Red Wheel/Weiser, LLC
With offices at:
665 Third Street, Suite 400
San Francisco, CA 94107
www.redwheelweiser.com

ISBN: 978-1-61852-049-4

Cover design by Jim Warner

Printed in the United States of America

10 9 8 7 6 5 4 3 2 1

Dedication

For my golden goddesses, Maddie and Serena—may you fearlessly walk the less trodden pathways, or better yet . . . create your own.

For my heart-sisters who have supported me every step of the way—you are a grace in my life.

And for Leif, with immense love and gratitude.

Contents

"A human being has so many skins inside, covering the depths of the heart. We know so many things, but we don't know ourselves! Why, thirty or forty skins or hides, as thick and hard as an ox's or bear's, cover the soul. Go into your own ground and learn to know yourself there."

—Meister Eckhart

Acknowledgments

Sherry Folb, my editor extraordinaire—you have helped me immeasurably. Your attention to every detail, along with your sound advice, has produced a book I am thrilled to share with others. Sabrina Rood, your final edits were astute and thoughtful. I thank you so much.

Sasha, and Navya, thank you for reading each chapter I sent to you. Your feedback was galvanizing and incredibly helpful. You fed my courage to keep putting myself out there. I cherish your friendship.

Amelia, I am so grateful. You midwifed me through the writing of this book and everything I experienced on every level. You are my sister of the heart.

Richard, I thank you for your generosity of heart and all that we have learned together.

My beautiful Leif, you came into my life as a friend, then a lover and a catalyst of such immense force I am forever changed. You remain in my heart as my brother who has journeyed with me over lifetimes. I will hold you dear for always.

Psychedelic Advisory

This book shares my personal experience and opinions on the use of sacred mushroom medicine. It is not intended as a substitute for medical or professional advice and should be used for educational and informational purposes only. Psilocybin mushrooms are still illegal substances in the United States and are not to be taken lightly. The psychedelic experience can be powerfully transformative or destructive. Readers who wish to make their own exploration of sacred medicine should consult with a qualified practitioner or medical professional.

The author and publisher specifically disclaim any responsibility for the results of any use of sacred mushroom medicine.

Prologue

My Shamanic Roots

I think religious hierarchies are very unsettled by the idea of direct revelation. Nevertheless, this phenomenon is certainly thriving in pre-literate cultures all over the world. We discovered in dealing with this that the only people you could talk to about it or who seemed to have familiarity with it were shamans.

—Terence McKenna, *Archaic Revival*

Our highly dysfunctional culture, with its overwhelming emphasis on materialism, serves only to keep us disconnected from our true selves. I have been a willing participant in this culture, spending half my life as a New Yorker under the spell of the city. I was always wanting more, desperately trying to fill a bottomless inner chasm, and like many I was seduced by the external forces all around me.

It wasn't until I was dragged kicking and screaming to Seattle that I began to journey deeply inward. I arrived bitter and resentful, homesick for my friends and the life I had in New York, where I had a busy social schedule. Then my marriage collapsed.

This was the classic face-slap that wakes us from our stupor. I was in excruciating pain, and I knew enough to know that the pain was an indication that I was in a major life transition.

I began daily meditation and journaling, reading book after book on spirituality and consciousness. Also at this time I was experiencing subtle energy waves that would move from my genital area to my stomach at night when I lay down to sleep.

A year or so later I met Richard and was thrilled to meet an attractive, accessible man who was also a passionate spiritual seeker. It was through Richard that I met Dr. Brugh Joy, who became one of my spiritual teachers. I attended his ten-day foundational teaching and then signed up for his yearlong study group, which threw me into in-depth shadow work. Up until then, I knew nothing of shadow, and now I was working with a master of it.

I then discovered Tom Kenyon, an acoustic brain research scientist, sound healer, shaman, and channel, who also became my teacher. Tom, like Brugh, is a heretic, rejecting dogma and challenging religious and social mores. He is funny, irreverent, and *human*, and is a master of sound. Working with these teachers opened me to a profound, in-depth exploration of consciousness, and I have been a devoted seeker ever since.

My shamanic side came forward during the ten-day session with Brugh in the Arizona desert. Part of the experience was to do three days of fasting and silence. I couldn't wait to get out into the desert. Once there, I searched for a place off the path, where I had decided I would create a circle. I knew nothing of medicine wheels at that time, nor had I made any kind of exploration into shamanism. I was just acting on what was coming through me. Later I came into an awareness of a group of grandmothers who were guiding me at that time.

I searched for rocks for this circle, my intention being to create something I could sit or lie down in for the next few days. All around me were cacti called "jumping cactus." They have this name because when you brush past them, they send out a little piece of cactus full of barbed thorns that catches you somewhere on your body and hurts like hell. Despite the fact that I was supposed to be in silence, it was broken frequently with a harshly whispered, "MotherFUCKER!" After that, their scientific name as far as I was concerned was "motherfuckers."

Once the circle was complete, I knew that it needed an "X." Again, I had no knowledge of creating the Four Directions—it just came in as an X, so I went with it. Later, I realized this is an equidistant cross representing the Four Directions. I was told that it must be made with little white stones. Of course, they were in short supply, and it was in that moment that I wondered if maybe this was some kind of an initiation. After a while I had found enough of those stones to create my X, all the while undergoing frequent attacks from the motherfuckers surrounding me.

Before I stepped into my circle, I received that I had to "wake it up." I stepped inside and began to slap the ground, drawing up energy from the earth with my hands and calling it upward. Then I stood up with my hands to the sky and asked the sky to open and shower my circle. I called in spirits from the desert and when I felt it was complete, I sat down. I didn't realize until later that I had just opened up a vortex. I took a seat in the circle as one person, and two days later, I would leave it as a shaman/priestess initiate.

No sooner had I sat down than one more motherfucker stuck to my forearm. Without a moment's hesitation I grabbed one of the stones framing the circle and smashed the shit out of a very tiny motherfucker growing nearby. And without thinking I cried silently to all of them, "If you do that one more time . . . I'll kill ALL your babies!"

I was a little taken aback by what I'd just done. I thought to myself that that wasn't very spiritual. What I realized later was that it was an initiation around claiming space. And from that time forward the motherfuckers never attacked me again. I returned to that circle four more times the following year when I came back to work with Brugh, and never, not once, did those motherfuckers jump me.

For the next couple of days I spent the entire day inside that circle, coming back to my room only at night to sleep. To my amazement, there was no end to what was possible in that circle. When I lay down in it, I felt the energy waves moving up from my genital area and into my third chakra. My entire body would proceed to quake and this would go on for as long as a couple of hours. I loved how it felt. At one point my entire body was beating like a heart. I felt initial panic at what was happening until a voice told me I was feeling the heartbeat of Mother Earth. I felt immense gratitude to be graced with that experience. It put me into a state of pure bliss.

Then the visions began and numerous goddesses visited me. I was offered an elixir from one goddess, and I drank it willingly with the understanding that this was an energetic imparting. I could actually feel a sensation of liquid entering my body.

By the time the fasting and silence was over, I was vibrating at a whole new level. When our group came back together to share about the experience, I shared what happened in my circle. Afterward, women from the group began approaching me, asking if they could experience being in the circle. We would stand inside and work with ritual. It was my first experience inducting women, portending what was to come. As time went on I became drawn more deeply into working with the shamanic realms and assisting women in accessing their own connection to their inner shaman/priestess.

When I returned home, I read Michael Harner's book, *The Way of the Shaman*, and ordered a drumming CD so that I could journey consistently. I took a shamanic weekend intensive that opened me more deeply. I was also guided to other teachers who taught techniques for journeying, divination, and healing.

One of those teachers was Miguel Angel Vergara, a Mayan priest and shaman. I was blessed to work with him one-on-one in the magical Yucatan, where ancient Mayan ruins beckoned me to walk among them. It was there that the Mayan mother goddess, Ix Chel, began to speak to me. That initiated another great change as I began to take on more of a role as teacher and ceremonialist.

Another shaman teacher I worked with, John Knowlton, came to our home for two years to teach a group of us. He taught us Peruvian shamanism, peppering it with his own brilliant insights and experiences. We would meet four weekends each year and we hungrily took in the teachings. This is where I put together my *mesa*, which is a medicine bundle that I use for healing and divination. That in-depth, experiential exploration of shamanism was a sacred gift for me. The teachers were actually coming to my house to teach me! I answered the call with all the integrity of my being.

As devoted to the practice of shamanism as I was, I was not interested in being an "Indigenous Person Wannabe."

I have always followed my own path, letting my heart lead me to the right teachers and experiences. Mine has been a journey of self-empowerment and it remains so today.

Plant spirit medicine was something I had been drawn to for a few years. Eventually, I had the opportunity to sit in an Ayahuasca ceremony with a circle of women with two female shamans leading. This had been a dream, as I had lamented a few months earlier about the dearth of female Ayahuascaros. Lo and behold, I got invited to my first Ayahuasca ceremony and it was led by two women.

The experience was incredible and I engaged the medicine a few more times after that. However, it didn't feel like it was my path. My friend, Leif, would often say that it's important to work with one's local medicine. I live in the moist, forested Pacific Northwest where mushrooms grow abundantly. It was the mushroom medicine that eventually called to me, and I see that plant as my greatest teacher.

Terence McKenna was a voice for the sacred mushroom for a number of years until his death in 2000. Although I do not resonate with some of his speculative views about various subjects, he did much for promoting the use of the sacred mushroom.

McKenna spoke about plant medicines being sanctioned, meaning they have been used by shamanic communities for thousands of years around the world and have not been shown to be dangerous. They certainly demand our respect, and substances like psilocybin have been abused egregiously in our culture. Plant medicine is a powerful tool for the expansion of consciousness, and the right use of these substances will shift the seeker in profound ways.

I knew that with the ceremonial use of the sacred mushrooms, I had found a most potent path in my shamanic exploration. Each journey offered me direct experience with the spirit realms. And more and more, I noticed how this world and the others were intersecting.

Introduction

It's not on any map. True places never are.
                    —Herman Melville, *Moby-Dick*

This story chronicles my journey into a profound awakening. It begins with the dissolution of a challenging marriage. It then moves into a series of highly transformative shamanic journeys with sacred plant medicine. I would never have imagined myself exploring these levels of consciousness so profoundly, but grace can bring us to the most numinous experiences.

As my marriage dissolved, an unexpected and powerfully beautiful relationship developed between two dear friends. It offered deep healing and transformation for me, even as it propelled me into a painful dark night of the soul.

Ultimately, this is the story of my journey into Self. It became necessary for me to fall in love with the mystery of my own being. With the failure of my marriage to Richard, I was called to explore the inner workings of my life patterns. It was time to mine my soul for the jewels of self-realization and expanded awareness.

My dissolving marriage was a powerful catalyst for this level of self-reflection. Marriage can serve as an activator for awakening us to a deeper knowing of ourselves. Ours was a blending of families and it was rife with personality conflicts. Rather than go into anger and blame, it became necessary for me to step outside the story as a fair witness to what was actually happening. I wanted to get to the bottom of my own life patterns that were repeating themselves in my relationships.

The unconscious forces of shadow and the life patterns struck at birth lead us to situations in life that offer us the chance to know ourselves very deeply. In addition, the opportunity to come into this level of self-knowledge has brought me humility and wisdom and has intensified my desire to be in service to life.

Native cultures talk about the importance of bringing into consciousness the life patterns that drive us. It is understood that if we make a pattern conscious and learn how to navigate through it, our children will not have to carry it. I feel a responsibility to my children as well as to myself to engage in this lineage work sincerely.

When we heal deep-seated inner wounds, when we address our shadow material and discover the patterns we've been living out unconsciously, we send an energetic healing through the time-space continuum. This healing goes backward through our ancestry and forward to our future generations. And as each of us takes responsibility for our own personal healing, we help to raise the vibration of the collective.

Carl Jung wrote, "The shadow is a moral problem that challenges the whole ego-personality, for no one can become conscious of the shadow without considerable moral effort. To become conscious of it involves recognizing the dark aspects of the personality as present and real. This act is the essential condition for any kind of self-knowledge and it therefore, as a rule, meets with considerable resistance."

I know that when I can embrace the totality of my being, the dark and the light, I can experience true wholeness. I can then maneuver myself through life with more mindfulness and maturity. Of course, getting myself to that place is no easy task. Relationships serve as mirrors, and if we don't like what is reflected back to us, it takes courage to search inward rather than point the finger outward. I have discovered that the intensity of my reaction and pain around a situation is directly relational to how much unresolved material I am holding within me.

My marriage to Richard revealed unconscious forces that had been running my entire life. It was the catalyst that brought me to my knees and forced me to acknowledge the parts within me that I project onto others. The further I held them from my awareness, the more pronounced they became in my life. The saying, "That which you resist, persists" is very apt here.

When I began engaging sacred plant medicine, my journey inward was taken to a whole new level. At one point in my exploration, I was able to confront and heal a core wound that had colored all my relationships. This wound fed my doubts about my worth as a person and my right to receive love. My healing came to me through a plant-medicine journey of such power and magnitude that I am forever changed. This healing was essential. It has enabled me to move forward, unburdened and unhindered by the past.

My experiences with the mushroom medicine have cultivated an intimate relationship with Mother Earth and a coterie of spirit beings. Through the use of sacred mushrooms, I have experienced an expansion of consciousness

I never thought possible. It has deepened my sense of belonging within a vast universe of countless realms. This medicine is a potent portal into the world of the spirits.

For thousands of years, shamans around the world have ingested psychotropic plant medicines—what we call psychedelics. These plants were used with reverence in sacred rituals. The intention was to bring back healing and guidance from the spirits. Ingesting the plant would take the shaman to an alternate reality where she would see and hear spirit beings that would communicate with her. Author Terence McKenna called this "ecstatic trance shamanism."

Our culture does not understand this. It views psychedelics as potentially dangerous and derelict, as something one may experiment with in high school or college and then discard in favor of more socially acceptable drugs like alcohol and pharmaceuticals. Those substances can be highly addictive and incredibly damaging. This is not true of psychotropic plants as they are not addictive. They will, however, illuminate the mind and sometimes bring forth challenging material for the user. It is very important that one learn as much as possible about the responsible and sacred use of psychotropic substances. To use the mushrooms as an escapist recreational drug denies the user the potent wisdom the fungus offers and profanes the mushrooms.

Psilocybin perturbs the brain, cracking open the psyche and shattering our perceptions of "reality." There is a palpable *other* within the medicine, known as a plant teacher. Unlike human teachers, the plant teachers do not possess the filters and biases we humans have when we bring through information. Plant teachers are pure, unadulterated spirit embodied, and they see right into the essence of our being.

My mystical experiences with the sacred mushrooms are woven throughout this book. In the telling of my journeys, I am endeavoring to share something that is quite difficult to convey in words. The experiences are profoundly mystical, as well as bizarre and, at times, hilarious. Each journey is unique and rich with imagery and felt experience.

Plant medicine is available to anyone who seeks a deeper life experience. There is no intermediary necessary. It is up to the individual to decide how to take the mushrooms. One must use personal discretion as to the quantity ingested, the intentionality, and any ceremony created around it. It is highly unfortunate that psilocybin mushrooms are illegal in the United States. They are in actuality expanders of consciousness and we would be well served to initiate a change of the laws concerning this misunderstood fungus. As adults and citizens of the Earth, we have every right to explore our own consciousness through the use of these substances.

My medicine journeys and my personal story are offered here, warts and all. It is my hope to inspire those intrepid souls who are not content to keep along the safe channels of what our culture offers. This is for the free-spirited ones who see beyond the regulated, sterile societal constructs and instead dare to explore the less trodden path. This is a path that leads one deeply into the ultimate mystery—the mystery and profundity of Self and our relationship to the All.

⬱ 1 ⬱

Beginnings

*I live on Earth at present and I don't know what I am. I
know that I am not a category. I am not a thing—a noun.
I seem to be a verb, an evolutionary process—an integral
function of the universe.*

—Buckminster Fuller

A t the age of six I led my first ritual. I was attending
a convent school run by nuns, and on the grounds
were the most magical evergreen trees. If you walked
underneath them it was like being in a teepee. I spent
many a recess under those trees. One day, I stole a nee-
dle from my mother's sewing kit and took my best friend,
Joanna, under the tree with me. I said a little prayer for
us and then pricked both our fingers and rubbed them
together, declaring us "Indian sisters."

How I knew to do that at such a young age is beyond
me, but I've never forgotten that experience. I had a vivid
imagination when I was young and was very comfortable
playing in my fantasy world with my fairy friends.

When I was a little older, I devoured a series of fairy-
tale books by Andrew Lang called *The Red Fairy Book, The*

Blue Fairy Book, and on and on by color. These were not modern Disney stories, but old fairy tales from all over the world, complete with the most beautiful drawings of nymphs and fairies and elves. Those stories stirred my imagination and I spent considerable time looking for those beings in my garden.

I also loved a large tree that stood regally in our front yard. I enjoyed hours just sitting on one of its branches, communing with the spirit of the tree. I never had an actual conversation with it because that was not how it talked to me. I simply felt it and it felt me, and that was enough. When my family had to move, I mourned that beautiful tree. We were good friends.

As I grew older I lost touch with this very special connection to the nature realms. I proceeded to assimilate into the cultural constructs that I never quite got the hang of. I spent my twenties living in the East Village in New York, waitressing, going to acting classes, and auditioning for roles that always got away from me.

I loved living in the city. My heart was in New York and I planned to live there the rest of my life. I used to say that in New York there was room for everyone. You could experiment with any way of being. You could be as banal or outrageous as you wished and no one would bat an eye. As someone who was willing to experiment with different expressions of being, I found this very appealing.

Eventually, I fell in love with a Wall Street guy. He was whip-smart, charismatic, and incredibly funny. My life changed dramatically. Suddenly I was eating at the restaurants I would have killed to get a job at. We travelled together often, seeking out cool places for scuba-diving adventures. Our home was a large loft in Soho that hosted many late-night soirées.

At that time I attended school for interior design and worked at that profession for the next several years. I was thrilled that I had the privilege of experiencing New York in such diverse ways. In my twenties, I was the starving actress, surviving in an East Village studio. In my thirties, I had season tickets to the ballet, I lived in beautiful homes that I decorated, and I had clients and friends whom I adored.

In my mid-thirties, we had two daughters, Maddie and Serena. I embraced motherhood with all the passion and love I had within me. I knew at that time that my own start in life had been unstable and I was determined to raise children who felt secure and loved from day one. Unfortunately, at this time things began to go sour in my marriage. The pressures began to cause tension and emotional distance. We were both becoming very unhappy with our circumstances, and our mutual disconnect grew ever wider.

Eventually, my husband decided to move us to Seattle, where he would start a small firm with a former business associate. I was devastated. I never wanted to leave New York. Seattle felt light-years away from the action and exuberance of the city. I remember at the time Alex Witchell of the *New York Times* declared Seattle a "Prada-free zone." I was certain I was being relegated to a D-list design no-man's-land.

In Seattle, everything changed. I lost my whole identity. In New York I had a tiny design firm that kept me very busy. I was president of the co-op board in my building, I had a great social life with friends I cherished, and I had a long-standing love affair with New York. Seattle had a very different groove, being much more laid-back and casual. People seemed friendly but they didn't socialize as easily as the New York crowd. I was alone constantly. Eventually we bought a large home in Capitol Hill and I threw myself into renovating and gardening.

At that point my marriage collapsed and I was about to become a forty-year-old single mother, which triggered every fear and insecurity I had. I was in incredible pain and it was at that time that I began to look inward. I was then gifted with a book by Don Miguel Ruiz called *The Mastery of Love*. This opened me to a whole new way of thinking and I began my spiritual journey inward. For the next year and a half I meditated daily. I worked with Tarot cards, experimenting with my oracular capacities. I read *A Course in Miracles* and then began consuming every book I could find on expanding consciousness. I gave myself over to a lifelong process of engaging Spirit, and I hoped to eventually find a partner with an expanded awareness.

To my great joy, I soon met Richard. Like me, he was a voracious spiritual seeker. He was warm and engaging and we became inseparable very quickly. We were together for seven years and married for five. Our relationship was at times wonderful and at other times incredibly difficult.

After a courtship of seven months, I moved in with Richard and his children. We became a blended family and that brought about huge challenges. Richard had custody of his children, a daughter, who was twelve at the time, and a son, fourteen. I had brought my two girls, who were four and seven.

Two people fall in love and come together with high hopes of forming a family that will adapt and coexist harmoniously. The statistics show that blended families have a divorce rate of 65 percent. Couple that with the fact that I was an opinionated, assertive New Yorker and Richard was an easygoing, casual West Coast guy, and you have a clash of cultures, among other things.

There is an excellent book on relationships called *Getting the Love You Want*, by Harville Hendrix, who developed Imago therapy. The therapy works on the premise that as we grow from baby to adult, our subconscious forms a composite of both positive and negative characteristics of our main caretakers. When we grow up and meet the person we feel a connection with, it is because the subconscious recognizes that person as possessing many of those traits. Essentially, the families we grow up in form the software for our future romantic relationships. We then enter relationship, hopefully to help each other heal and grow, but as most of this is unconscious, many of us end up re-wounding each other.

Imago therapy gives us an awareness of the wounds we received when we were younger and offers insight into how we can change our behavior with our partner to shift into a relationship that builds trust, partnership, and honoring. I did not have this level of insight going into my relationship with Richard. However, the therapy helped me examine my own role in the marriage.

As eager spiritual students, Richard and I studied and travelled with some amazing teachers. Our bond felt deeply spiritual and we felt our relationship to be brimming with potential. We saw ourselves teaching together in the future and eventually bought a large home so we could host various workshops and do our own teaching.

When one enters relationship, one does not arrive empty handed. We each bring our respective baggage, consisting of unresolved wounds from the past, survival tactics, and our ideas and opinions based on our life experiences. I was adopted, which had always haunted the back

of my mind with the idea that somehow I was a "mistake."
Add to that my feeling of not being taken seriously growing up, not feeling validated, always getting into trouble,
and in my mind being the "fuck-up."

I also had a sense of entitlement, with the rationale
that if someone isn't going to do it for me, then by God,
I'll do it myself and I'll make it happen. This can work for
me or against me. All of the above are things I've worked
on in the past; however, when triggered in highly emotional circumstances, I can go completely unconscious.
And without the astute insights of Hendrix's book, all
bets were off.

Each of us enters into relationship carrying our core
wounds. We then unconsciously engage the very forces
we encountered growing up, now cloaked in a different
person and situation. That's when the fun begins.

Richard had experiences growing up that caused him
to be incredibly self-sufficient and independent, with
his own sense of entitlement. He grew up arguing with
a brilliant father, which made him exceptionally adept at
countering whenever I made an opinionated statement,
which would then accelerate into a huge argument, both
of us not giving an inch, each striving to be "right." Myself
wanting validation, and Richard wanting to win and
crush—and this was *before* the shit hit the fan.

⤳ 2 ⤳

The Shit Hits the Fan

*You meet someone and you're sure you were lovers in a
past life. After two weeks with them, you realize why you
haven't kept in touch for the last two thousand years.*

—Al Clethen

Richard and I had vastly different parenting styles,
which created incredible problems as time went on.
Kids can destroy a marriage, and ours was put to a test
that was to become the most challenging experience of
my entire life. I learned a tremendous amount through
it all. However, being in the experience was pretty damn
difficult.

Richard's ex-wife had walked out on him and their
children the day after Christmas, three years before we
met. It was a devastating blow and the children ended up
in his custody. A plan was worked out with the ex-wife
and they settled into their new life, albeit with no ongoing
therapy for the kids. Richard felt tremendous guilt about
what happened and he overcompensated by giving them
no chores or limits. They were never expected to pick up
after themselves and Richard was not a disciplinarian in

any way. They spent a couple of evenings each week with their mother as well as every other weekend.

My girls and I moved into Richard's house with excitement about our new living situation. Neither Richard nor I was prepared for the clash of personalities that was to ensue. At first, his children were excited about his New York girlfriend and they seemed to like my daughters. Initially, I liked his children despite the fact that they were not the most engaging. They would spend hours at the computer or in front of the TV, often staying up past midnight. Food was left out, and dishes were left to sit in the sink.

His daughter, Claire, was not an easy person to get to know. She preferred to keep her cards close to her chest, which I could understand after what she went through a few years earlier. Until I showed up, Claire had had her dad to herself for three years. She was the only girl in the house and she had enjoyed a home where there was no mom present to make her pick up her stuff or help out in any way.

His son, Jack, was nice enough but mostly left to his own devices. He too enjoyed the luxury of doing what he wanted. In terms of raising children, Richard always liked to say, "Life will teach them!" My feeling was that as parents it's really our job to prepare them for life, but Richard didn't see it that way. He was left pretty much to his own devices growing up and loved to say that he turned out all right so the same should be true for his kids.

As time went on, a power struggle developed between Claire and me as I began to assert myself in our home. I was told by Richard not to make her clean up because her mother was very messy and he didn't want Claire to feel there was something wrong with that. The long and short of it is that my role as stepmother was very murky. His children were already well established in their personalities and habits and I had little say about them.

Stepparents are often in awkward positions when it comes to their stepchildren. Being in agreement on parenting is hugely important. Outside guidance from a family therapist can be a tremendous help. Unfortunately, we did not seek this and as his daughter grew into a teenager, the problems grew larger and much more serious.

When his daughter was fifteen, all the signs were present that we were going to be in for a difficult ride. At one point, I expressed concern to Richard about the collection of hard liquor bottles she had in her bedroom, pointing out that a fifteen-year-old girl should not be proudly displaying empty Jack Daniels bottles in her room. Allowing it was, in my mind, condoning it. My concerns were rebuffed with his reply that he had liquor bottles in his room as a teenager and nobody minded. He also repeated her claim that she brought them home from parties but she didn't actually drink the liquor.

It was those ridiculous replies that outraged me. We would begin to argue and Richard would then proceed to take inventory and discredit me, thereby shunning my concerns and any wisdom I might have to offer, telling me that this is my "stuff" to work out.

Herein lies the fruit of the lesson for me, which took me another four years to realize. I spoke earlier about my own sense of not being taken seriously growing up, of not feeling validated. Now I found myself in a situation where I believed I was bringing up a valid concern, pointing out something that had relevance, and not being acknowledged. I was certainly not being validated. At the same time, because it was a core issue for me, I was not exactly gentle in my approach, mixing assertion with aggression in the form of sarcasm and angry finger-pointing.

Without the awareness of how my own unhealed wounds were at play in this situation, I simply went into reaction, exacerbating the situation and making things worse for myself as a result.

This went on for three more years. My relationship with Claire had never been strong and we barely spoke, giving each other a wide berth as resentments grew on both sides. I wish I could say that I behaved with compassion and loving-kindness, but I did not. I was furious with her behavior and the way she flaunted her ability to do whatever she wanted without impunity. I was also concerned for my girls, who were much younger. I did not want them to be exposed to her creepy friends, the alcohol, and the awful way she spoke to her father.

Claire was clearly crying out for help, but none came. Her rage was on her sleeve at every turn and I was at a loss at how to handle it. Her father would not put her in therapy, saying she was too stubborn to cooperate, which was probably true. My input was not wanted and yet I continued to raise the red flag when I saw the train rushing in.

I was hotly disliked by Richard's kids because I was the "bad guy" who was constantly requesting limits for them. Their father preferred the role of "friend dad," desiring to be liked by the kids and their friends. He did not want to come down on them in any way. He felt that I was bullying and judgmental, and he rejected my demands to reel in his kids.

By that time I was teaching workshops and hosting monthly full-moon ceremonies for women. A good friend at the time said to me, "It's poignant that so many women are drawn to you for your wisdom but your own husband doesn't want to hear any of it."

That was heartbreaking to me. Yet how could he hear it when by this time, my approach with him had deteriorated to raw annoyance and anger? We were not partners when it came to his children. Even though they lived in our house, it was understood that Richard and his ex would handle any disciplinary issues, and of course, in my mind, this was rarely if ever addressed. So a gulf of resentment and hurt widened between us.

After two serious incidents, specific measures were taken to get Claire the help she needed. It was at that time that I wanted to leave the marriage. I was done. I had been incredibly lonely. Richard felt the same way, both of us feeling alone and misunderstood. We were battle weary and damaged by angry words.

At that time I had no escape route. I was miserable and utterly stuck. With two girls it was not so easy to simply up and leave. I was building my teaching and wouldn't be ready to move out for a good while.

During that time I was involved in a two-year shamanic intensive. Four weekends out of each year, a group of ten of us would converge on our house to go deeply into experiential teachings using the energies of the Four Directions. I was also working with a shaman and Mayan priest in the Yucatan. In addition, I was channeling a group of grandmothers and bringing through transmissions from the Mayan Earth Mother, Ix Chel. I felt like I had found what I'd searched for my whole life. My dedication to shamanic practices got me through that very difficult time. I meditated or journeyed every day, often seeking counsel from the ancestors to help me through.

Richard and I continued to stay together, but our relationship never recovered. I threw myself into my teaching and writing, deepening my connection to the spirit realms. My girls had weathered the difficult times, which was a relief. I had chosen to keep them abreast of the various incidents that had occurred, using them as a teaching opportunity, and it worked. As a result, my girls felt secure. Each of them thanked me for being honest and straightforward about the events that occurred. Our relationships remain steadfast and close today.

Claire eventually moved in with her mother. Richard's adult son was still around, his bedroom located at the other end of our home. I had my own issues with him, but Richard protected him with the ferocity of a papa bear. My last big fight with Richard was over a series of incidents regarding his son. The fight was terrible, and for over a month we did not talk. This may seem extreme, but after years of this kind of thing, the resentment was huge, and coming back to each other was no easy thing. During that time I knew that the marriage was truly over. And yet a part of me still clung to the hope that we might possibly be able to work things out.

At the end of that month I took the initiative and apologized sincerely to Richard. My apology was met with relief. We talked for a while and decided to come back together, albeit gingerly.

The following day I was to receive an astrological relationship reading for Richard and myself by a most gifted astrologist and intuitive, Alisha Michell. Her reading was very insightful and she had both of us pegged. As an intuitive myself, I knew she was holding back. I knew she could see that we were not going to be together much longer. I knew it and yet I decided I would give it one last shot.

Richard and I listened to the reading together, which was very helpful. Alisha was able to point out certain things about us that we would not have been able to hear from each other. The reading put much into perspective in terms of our personality traits, our patterns, and our karmic agreements.

As a practicing shaman, I felt the obvious next step was to do some kind of ceremony to assist our coming back together in a spirit of integrity and sincerity. This would be done with the intention of bringing our negative impulses into the light.

To support us I called in the spirits and we did a fire ceremony. I suggested we sit down and write each other a love letter that we then read out loud. We spent the weekend together and wrote up a contract detailing how we would relate from that time forward.

And all the king's horses and all the king's men . . .

No matter how powerful the ritual, no matter how well intentioned, it would ultimately not be enough to bring us back together.

☙ 3 ❧

In Retrospect

Tears, sorrow, and disappointment are bitter, but wisdom is the comforter in all psychic suffering. Indeed, bitterness and wisdom form a pair of alternatives: where there is bitterness wisdom is lacking, and where wisdom is there can be no bitterness.

—Carl Jung, *Mysterium Coniunctionis*

During those challenging years when I was married to Richard, I lamented as to why I did not have the means to get out when I wanted out. My feeling has always been that until the lesson is learned, the issue will keep repeating itself. So I had to ask myself: *What is it I am not getting here? What do I have to learn that is obviously so critical I am being held in place till I get it?*

My personal process of self-discovery is shared to inspire curiosity rather than dread when it comes to facing our cast-out material. When situations repeat themselves in our lives, it is a wake-up call to address the deeper forces within us. It can be frightening to explore ourselves this deeply. That fear is the indication that we are approaching a growth edge that is going to take us to a whole new level of awareness if we will just trust the process.

One of my students told me about a wonderful therapist who was a shaman in her own right. This therapist had a practice based on Imago therapy and was very good. My student credited this woman with saving her marriage and empowering her and her husband to heal. I had known that my marriage to Richard was going to end, but I initiated the therapy for us in the hopes that we could get to the bottom of our issues once and for all. I wanted to carry these lessons into a future relationship with the hope that I would be a more conscious partner.

This began an exploration into my own history from birth through my teen years, where the relational patterns were established. A critical "aha'" for me was after Richard had said to me recently, "You've become a much better person since we've been together."

I remember thinking, *Hmmm. I guess that's what a compliment sounds like from someone with an element of superiority.* Then I remembered something my ex-husband had said to me along the same lines.

In this case, it felt like Richard was taking credit for me somehow becoming a "better person" since we'd been together. But the similarity was too pronounced to ignore. So, I wondered, *Why have I attracted men who see me as someone they need to fix?*

It occurred to me that part of my relational patterning was formed during my adolescence and teen years. I had a difficult relationship with my mother, who could not relate to who I was at the time. I internalized her frustration with me to mean that I was a constant disappointment and even an embarrassment to her. I took her criticisms to heart, along with the guilt and shame I felt at not being the model daughter.

Lo and behold, one of the things I experienced in each of the two major relationships of my life was a lot of criticism from my mates. And, of course, I could dish it out too. My ex-husband was quite forthright in his criticisms of me. Richard, too, was quick to list my faults in our fights, as well as in the ensuing emails we would shoot back and forth.

I realized I had long ago internalized and cemented my feelings of not being good enough, of not measuring up. In so doing, I unconsciously attracted consistent judgment from the men in my life. That which is unconscious can run us very easily. Until we recognize the patterns, we are slaves to them.

There was also shadow material for me to explore. This was an opportunity to go within and find out what I'd disowned. These men were reflecting back to me a part of myself. When I thought about it, I realized that within me is a masculine authority that constantly judges. This inner masculine authority is never satisfied. He is the ultimate taskmaster, driving me to do as much as I can to prove my worth.

Part of bringing these shadow pieces to light involves redeeming them. My teacher, Brugh Joy, would ask, "What's right about the judgmental masculine authority? How does he serve?"

Our first impulse is to reject our shadow material as something to be ashamed of or embarrassed about. Brugh would say that these unconscious parts are but a clump of trees in the forest of our being. They do not define us. However, if we do not own them, they will own us. Once we bring these shadow pieces into the light, it removes the charge associated with them.

So how does this judgmental masculine serve me? He keeps me self-disciplined and keeps me responsible. He also helps me with discernment. If I integrate him, he no longer runs me unconsciously and I no longer have to make someone else carry him for me. I can catch myself when I go into judgment, particularly harsh judgment. This enables me to reel myself in and own what's my responsibility to own. Just knowing that piece lives in me makes it much easier to shift.

A great quote by Jung comes from his book, *Psychology and Religion*. It states, "Unfortunately, there can be no doubt that man is, on the whole, less good than he imagines himself or wants to be. Everyone carries a shadow, and the less it is embodied in the individual's conscious life, the blacker and denser it is. If an inferiority is conscious, one always has a chance to correct it. Furthermore, it is constantly in contact with other interests, so that it is continually subjected to modifications. But if it is repressed and isolated from consciousness, it never gets corrected and is liable to burst forth suddenly in a moment of unawareness. At all events it forms an unconscious snag, thwarting our most well-meant intentions."

There is an important self-love piece around shadow work as well. When we re-integrate a part of ourselves that was unloved, we increase our capacity to love ourselves more fully.

Looking at my role in this marriage, I had to own my inner struggle with power and powerlessness. I like to be in control, and when confronted with other family members who had no interest in the environment I wanted to create, I went to the extreme end of control. This created an equal and opposite energy, sending those around me into full-scale rebellion. The harder I pushed for them to be compliant, the more they went in the opposite direction. If I could have just pulled back and relaxed my hold on controlling, it would have allowed those around me to also pull back from rebellion.

At the same time, my efforts to maintain order in the home and have Richard discipline his kids caused Richard to be even more passive with them. I was the hard-ass and he was the softie. We each carried what the other wouldn't.

It has been an eye-opening gift to have the opportunity to examine my role in co-creating this dynamic between Richard, his kids, and me. I really believe that relationships are modern-day mystery schools. I entered into a sacred temple of alchemy with the person I fell in love with and we became a mirror for each other. Old wounds were triggered, shadow material came forward, and the process of shaping and growing began. Depending on how rigorously self-honest I am, I can evolve myself in leaps and bounds. A great many people go into victim and blame in relationships. Certainly when our deepest hurts are triggered, it is very easy to go into anger and blame with all the self-righteousness we can muster.

I was finally getting how critical it was to look inward. Doing so would enable me to make the necessary changes so I could greet another with consciousness. My relationship with Richard had run its course and, rather than devolve into anger and blame, I chose to glean all the self-awareness I possibly could.

The Imago therapy was incredibly helpful in showing me the roots of Richard's behaviors as well. That freed me from taking so much of it personally. It really wasn't my job to examine him. As Brugh Joy used to say, "It's not OUT there! It's in HERE," pointing to himself.

My relationship with Richard, although tremendously challenging, has also resulted in my coming to the place I am now. I have grown exponentially in the alchemical fires of that relationship. It has not been easy, but it has been a necessary container to develop and expand my soul.

The formal dissolution of our marriage didn't happen till the fall. After resolving our latest fight, I entered into a series of life-changing experiences that shook me to the core of my being. My life would never be the same again.

❧ 4 ❧

A Heroic Dose

*The overwhelming effect of the night under the influence
of an hallucinogen gives natural birth to a feeling of shared
supernatural experience never to be forgotten, a feeling of
cofradia, of brotherhood. Those who pass through a velada,
in the right set and setting, live through an awesome experience, and feel welling up within them a tie that unites them
with their companions of that night of nights that will last
for as long as they live.*
—Carl A.P. Ruck, R. Gordon Wasson, Albert Hofmann,
The Road to Eleusis: Unveiling the Secret of the Mysteries

Immediately after Richard's and my ritual to begin again,
I was scheduled to take a trip north to stay at the home
of a mutual friend of ours. Leif had been part of our two-
year shamanic intensive and I considered him a trusted
friend. We had a very clear connection—we really got
each other. There were a number of times when he would
call about something he was researching and I had just
finished watching a documentary on that very subject. We
were on a similar wavelength and I found it comforting
to know someone who was as awake as he was. He was

extremely funny and irreverent, which I just loved. He was also very attractive, which was a nice bonus.

Earlier in the year I had expressed to Leif my desire to experience a journey on the sacred mushrooms. I could actually feel the medicine calling to me. I'd participated in Ayahuasca ceremonies, so I had direct experience with the profound inner shift that was possible on plant medicine. Intuitively I knew there was something for me to explore with the mushrooms. Leif had quite a bit of experience with plant medicines and he lived on a beautiful piece of property in a natural setting that was ideal for that type of ceremony. He had a deep reverence for the natural world and was very connected to the Earth.

We had chosen a weekend in July for me to come to his place and experience the medicine. I was to stay for a few days, hanging out and enjoying the beauty of the land. My girls were away with their father, which worked out perfectly.

Leif had been reading Terence McKenna, who wrote prolifically on plant medicines. McKenna had an encyclopedic knowledge of botany, history, philosophy, and mathematics. He spoke of the importance of approaching plant medicine with the same reverence as the shamans. Medicinal mushrooms had been debased in our modern culture by casual thrill-seekers. Those people lacked both understanding and respect for what is an ancient and sacred portal into expanded states of consciousness. McKenna felt that in order to experience the full depth of the medicine, one should do a "heroic dose" consisting of five grams of dried mushrooms. He advocated doing this lying down alone in the dark.

We would be taking the medicine at night outside on Leif's land, under a circular tent-like structure where we would put out sleeping bags and blankets. Our ceremony wouldn't begin till almost eleven, as it gets dark much later in the Pacific Northwest. I took a "disco nap" earlier in the evening while Leif created sacred space for our ceremony.

When it was time to begin, I walked out to our medicine area and was struck by the care Leif had put into creating a sacred space. Candles were lit. There was a pot of mushroom tea with two cups sitting between our mesas. My mesa had been missing a tie to keep it together, and I saw that he had wrapped it with a beautiful beaded rope for me.

We sat down and talked for a bit while we drank the mushroom tea. It wasn't the greatest tasting brew, but it was light-years better than the bitter Ayahuasca I had imbibed in the past. We then lay down a couple of feet apart and waited for the medicine to take hold.

After about thirty minutes or so I was bombarded by the most extraordinary images. Tiny elf-like beings were coming out of flowers and geometric shapes. They were everywhere. I saw a vast and beautiful spaceship above me that was whirling with colors and shapes. The imagery was relentless. My brain was trying to make sense of what I was seeing, but it was actually painful to try to "think" through what was being shown. This was a language of visuals and light. All I could do was settle back and watch. There was no trying to intellectualize or format what I was seeing as it was coming in too fast. It was the most amazing visionary spectacle I had ever seen.

Throughout the journey I was utterly incapacitated and I would find myself going in and out of consciousness. While this was happening, Leif had realized he wasn't really feeling much of the medicine and was fairly lucid. He was talking to me and I remember marveling how he could even hold a conversation as I was falling deeply into a whole other realm. He checked in with me at one point and I recall feeling nauseous. *I told him I wasn't doing so well, which was true in that I was very, very deep in the journey and it was overwhelmingly intense. Leif proceeded to go into caretaker mode, bringing me something to vomit in should I need it. At one point I awoke to him spritzing me with rosewater.*

It's funny to think about that now and also very touching.

At one point he told me he was running to the house for something and I felt a moment of panic at being left alone. It was at that exact moment that the medicine actually spoke to me.

It said, "Shonagh. Calm down. Let me be your teacher." I was not expecting this and I snapped back into the journey. A few minutes later I felt like I was being shaken apart energetically. My body wasn't moving, but it was almost as if an energetic overlay that was in my field was being electrified away. It felt like there was an electrical adjustment of some sort going on within me.

During the journey I saw a glimpse of the part of me that was terrified of losing control. I saw an image of myself as "good girl" in my Catholic-school uniform screaming to myself, "We can't DO this! This is CRAZY!" Of course, it was far too late for that sentiment. I let her fry away with the rest of my programming.

The journey lasted around five hours. Toward the end of the night I came out of it momentarily and saw that I was holding hands with Leif. I had been so deep in the hyperspace of the medicine that his hand felt like my connection with the "real" world. As I began to come back to this reality, his hand felt like a kind of lifeline to me and I was deeply touched by his kind attentiveness. When I would look at our hands I saw delicate, feathered wings that were simply beautiful.

When we finally began to talk I felt the strangest sensation of a very powerful emotion rising in me. I had the image of a beaker of water with a big bubble of oil hurtling upward from the bottom. I said out loud, "I feel emotion!" All of a sudden I was overcome with sobs. I cried like I haven't cried in years. I turned away from Leif and sobbed into the grass.

A few moments later I felt Mother Earth speak to me, "Daughter, cry your tears to me."

I'd recently had a conversation with someone who was saying that we really shouldn't be sending our negative emotions into the Earth to transmute because she's taken so much abuse; it only adds more stress to her.

So I said, "No. It's too much."

"My daughter, cry your tears to me. I can hold them."

Those words surprised me and I sobbed my heart into her. I began to key into an old wound I rarely thought about. I was adopted when I was five months old and the thought came into my head that I was a mistake. No sooner had the thought hit me than Mother Earth said with authority, "My daughter, you were NO mistake."

That made me cry even more as I felt her healing come into me. We proceeded to have a conversation and at one point I apologized for "my people" and how unconscious they were.

"Daughter, you are a teacher. Keep teaching your people. They will come to you."

During the night I was in no position to move around, and I had heard stories of male shamans who had helped themselves sexually to women who were on Ayahuasca. I realized how vulnerable I was in that state, lying next to Leif the entire night. He was ever respectful and kind. He took care of me when he thought I was having difficulty, and when we held hands, he did not take it as any kind of sexual invitation. I was safe with him and the trust I had in him was cemented after that night.

As we sat looking at the trees in front of us, I told him how grateful I was for his friendship. We talked about our regard for each other and at one point I said to him, "I love you like the trees. I love you with an old, ancient love the Earth has for her trees." It was spontaneous and from my heart. My entire being was opened as a result of the profound journey I'd just experienced. I felt immense gratitude to have someone like Leif in my life. He expressed his love for me and we sat there, surrounded by moss-covered trees, at peace in the stillness.

At some point, I turned to look at his house and I observed the moss he'd placed along the wraparound porch railing. I took in all the crystals and driftwood on the deck. It occurred to me that he lived in a fairy cottage. I turned to tell him when I saw that his face was replaced with the face of Pan! I blinked my eyes and when I looked at everything else around me, it all looked normal. I looked back at Leif and the face of Pan was looking back at me—goatee, pointy ears, horns, and all.

"Holy shit, you're PAN! I knew it! That makes perfect sense! And you live in a fairy cottage, for crying out loud!" I laughed hysterically at this realization. My dear, crazy friend, Leif, who was so deeply connected to the Earth, possessed the aspect of Pan, the god of the nature spirits! It was perfect! For a good hour, every time I looked at him, his face was the face of Pan. Everything else was normal except his face. Over the course of the next several months, Pan would continue making his presence known to me in the most extraordinary ways.

As I walked toward the house to the bathroom, I had the distinct sensation that there was another being inside me. I got to the door and when I opened it, there were no lights on, only the fireplace burning. In the bathroom, Leif had left a lit candle. I was struck again by his caring attention in creating a peaceful, sacred space.

In the bathroom mirror I saw my face reflecting pure joy. My hands went to my heart chakra and I just stared at my happy face. All of a sudden, I saw my eyes change and my face rapidly took the shape of a mountain lion. I glanced at my hands and saw two giant paws over my chest. This was not a soft, blurry image, but a totally real mountain lion staring back at me. I felt the spirit of the cat inside me and realized that that was what I felt when I was walking up to the house.

As I backed slowly away from the mirror, I was stunned at the face looking back at me. I walked through the house feeling this feline spirit within me studying the surroundings. I made my way back to our ceremony space, all the while aware of mountain lion's presence within me.

I then told Leif what had happened, saying that the lion was actually an animal totem of mine I hadn't worked with in a couple of years. A few years earlier, I had attended a shamanic retreat and we were to do a journey to find our power animal. We were partnered with someone we didn't know and they were to make the journey for us to find our animal.

The night before that class I'd had a dream where I was being stalked by two lions on either side of my house. If I went one direction around the house, a lion would appear, and if I went the other direction, another lion would appear. I thought it was an interesting dream to have right before an immersion into shamanism, and I wrote it down.

When my partner came out of her journey, she whispered in my ear that she'd found a lion. I showed her my journal with the dream and we were both amazed. I had not worked much with the lion since then, but now I felt it engaging me very powerfully.

Something had cracked open for me that night. The mushrooms had opened a door to realms of consciousness that were as real as anything in this world, but they were unseen in waking consciousness. An intelligent, compassionate voice had spoken to me and offered me healing. McKenna had referred to this voice as "other" or "logos." I later read that plant medicines were also called *entheogens*, meaning "becoming divine within" or "generating the divine within."

I began researching to learn more about sacred mushroom medicine. Mexican Indians, who have used the mushrooms in sacred ritual for countless generations, have said this medicine will "carry you to where God is." The Aztecs used mushrooms in sacred ritual, referring to the fungi as "God's flesh."

These cultures understood that this medicine was a portal to transcendent, mystical states. Shamans who took this medicine brought back guidance and healing for their communities. Many of these cultures kept the mushrooms a well-guarded secret, feeling that if the medicine got into the wrong hands it would lose its magical powers.

Now I count myself as one of the fortunate few who have experienced a transcendental state that has opened my heart and spoken to my soul. It would not be my last, as this medicine had now become my teacher and my portal to the realms of Spirit.

⁓ 5 ⁓

Reverberations

Already things are changing; it's starting with small shit but oh it's starting, the change, the irrevocable, impossible change.
    —Suzanne Finnamore, *Split: A Memoir of Divorce*

When I arrived home from that weekend I knew I was forever changed. I had experienced direct engagement with Spirit and I had a felt sense of deep connection to the Earth. I knew this medicine was my teacher and I intended to work with it as often as I could. My path of shamanism was to include the use of plant spirit medicine, both for my own illumination and healing and for my community.

A few days later, Leif came by the house to pick up something I'd ordered for him. He hung out for a bit and we sat on the steps in front of my driveway. At some point, Richard's son, Jack, drove past us and into the garage. He never even glanced our way. He was in his own world, as usual.

The following day Richard came into my office to chat. I mentioned that Leif had been by and said to say hello. Richard said, "Oh, *that's* who Jack was talking about." I asked him what he meant and he said, "Jack asked 'Who was the guy holding hands with Shonagh in the driveway?'"

I felt my skin prickle with rage and I made myself breathe. I had caught Jack at something just over a month ago and he was furious with me for exposing him. I knew exactly what he was doing now.

"Don't you see the manipulation in that statement?" I asked. "It's kind of absurd that I would stand in the driveway holding hands with another man. I think Jack is wanting to get me back for what happened last month."

"Well, maybe you were handing something to Leif and it looked like you were holding hands. After all, Jack doesn't have a history of making up stories like that."

I stood there incredulous, as I had been so many times before when I heard Richard's rationalizations for his kids' behavior. Jack was never one to let the truth get in the way of a good story and Richard certainly wasn't going to question.

In that moment time stopped and a voice in my head said, "He cannot hear you. He will not hear you. Leave it alone. It's over."

That was the defining moment for me and I knew we were done.

I did not have the courage to tell Richard right away, and I knew dissolving the marriage would be a long haul. We were to begin the Imago therapy that week. When I talked to my shaman teacher about it, he said that Hendrix's book was one of the best books out there on relationship. He told me to go to the therapy despite the fact that the marriage was over, saying I would learn much about myself.

For the next six weeks, my focus was on my girls, my teaching, exploring my role in my marriage, and figuring out when I could get back to Leif's to experience the medicine again. The first weekend in August was to be my first time teaching a medicine-wheel intensive. A group of women had committed to work with me for the next year, meeting quarterly for a long weekend. I was very excited about it and I threw myself into creating an amazing class.

At the same time, I was thinking a lot about my friendship with Leif. I sought out my friend, Alisha, the astrologer, to see if she would do a relationship chart for us. I was curious to see what connections we shared. I was knocked a bit sideways by the feelings I was having for him and I was very conflicted. My entire life, I had never, ever been unfaithful to a man. And I'd never even dated a man who had a girlfriend, much less one who was married.

When I was going through the worst of the worst with Richard, it never even occurred to me to run into the arms of someone else. I had a lot of my own judgments around cheating. It was dawning on me that life was sweeping in to give me a lesson here. I had judged Richard's ex-wife harshly for cheating on him.

When Alisha put our charts together, she told me we were strongly connected in the eighth house of the astrology wheel, the house of the shaman and the mystic. That was nice to hear and no surprise. She then told me our charts showed a powerful soul-mate connection. When I was with Leif, I was totally at ease. We had a great banter and there was always laughter. I felt we were cut from the same cloth but I simply never thought of him in a romantic sense. I was married, after all, and on top of that, he was quite a bit younger.

Then Alisha said something that gave me chills. She said, "Your 'Eros,' which is your love, is in Capricorn, which is *Pan.*"

I didn't even know what to say to that. Alisha explained that it meant our love is very earthy and sensual and deep. She told me our charts indicated a deep soul bond, saying we would be friends for life and most probably lovers. I was shocked to hear this, yet it confirmed what I already knew in my heart. I let myself sit with this for the next few weeks.

I was very intrigued with this Pan energy that seemed to be figuring prominently for us. Leif carried that energy strongly. My knowledge of Pan was that he was the king of the nature spirits. He was playful and sensual and wise. I had a sense he was calling me to him.

What happened during my medicine-wheel training made this crystal clear. For the training I had planned to do a fire ceremony with my students. One of the women asked if she could take photos during the ceremony. I thought that would be fine, so I gave my consent.

Sheila took photos of the ceremony and our beautiful fire, and sent them to me that night. There were about four or five photos of the actual fire along with the ceremony pictures. I chose a few photos of our ceremony and quickly picked out a fire photo and emailed them off to Leif. Later, he sent back a message saying he loved the face in the fire. I had no idea what he was talking about, so I checked the photos, and when I looked at the fire photo I almost fell off my chair.

The fire was in the shape of a face and it was the face of Pan! The detail was so incredible it looked like it was photo-shopped. His entire profile was outlined perfectly with the nose, the lips, and the beard. There was an eye in the fire *exactly* where an eye should be and there was even a horn at the top of his head. I showed my medicine students the photo the next day and they were amazed. It now sits on my altar and Pan has become an ever-present spirit for me.

A week later a fortuitous synchronicity happened. I was planning to get back to Leif's for a medicine weekend in late August, when I ran into a friend and shared my mushroom experience. She proceeded to tell me that she had just worked with a strain of mushrooms that were from Palenque, in the Yucatan.

A year before that, I was in the Yucatan working one-on-one with my shaman teacher. We talked about doing sacred mushrooms together but had to forgo it because of an increased number of police checkpoints in the area. My teacher wisely chose not to risk it but he said to me, "Shonagh, just know that you don't find the medicine. The medicine finds you."

In that moment, the Maya medicine found me. I gave Leif a call with the news.

≈ 6 ≈

Maya Medicine

The short, stout, elder woman with her laughing moon face, dressed in a huipil, the long dress, embroidered with flowers and birds of the Mazatec women, a dark shawl wrapped around her shoulders, her gray hair parted down the middle and drawn into two pigtails, golden crescents hanging from her ears, bent forward from where she knelt on the earthen floor of the hut and held a handful of mushrooms in the fragrant, purifying smoke of copal rising from the glowing coals of the fire, to bless them: known to the ancient Meso-Americans as the Flesh of God, called by her people the Blood of Christ.

—Henry Munn, *The Mushrooms of Language*
From: *Hallucinogens and Shamanism*, Michael J.
Harner, ed.

I had a limited time to spend with Leif so we chose to do the medicine the night of my arrival. This time we opted to do it in a more forested area of his land, where the moss covered the ground and hung from the tree branches. It felt very Avalon-like and you could sense the presence of fairies everywhere.

We looked around for just the right place to do our ceremony. I saw a particularly beautiful grove of trees that had grown together on a mound. There was something very special about that grove and at one point I walked up to it and climbed to the base of one of the trees. I'd brought a crystal as an offering to the land and I placed the crystal in the base of two of the trees. I pressed my body into the tree and sent in my heart's light, finishing with a gentle kiss to the tree. When I looked down, Leif had been watching me and had tears in his eyes. I felt us in that moment as kindred spirits. I loved him and was deeply touched by his sensitivity.

We set up our ceremony area in a little clearing near the magical grove of trees. Because the mushrooms were from Palenque, I had decided to do a Mayan ceremony to lead us into the journey. I wore a long white dress, which is the color my teacher taught me to wear when doing ceremony. We set up our blankets and pillows and collected wood for a ceremonial fire. We would return just before dark to begin.

As darkness fell, we made our way to the ceremonial space. As we approached, Leif pointed upward to the branch of a tree and whispered, "Check it out. It's an owl."

Looking up, I could see the shadowy outline of a large owl. Earlier that month I had been on Gabriola Island in Canada with my girls. My eldest daughter and I had gone for a walk and came within twenty-five feet of a large barred owl perched on a fence post. It was the closest I'd ever come to an owl in the wild; he regarded us for several minutes, which was pure magic.

Here in the forest was an owl again. This one felt like an underworld guardian, welcoming us. We walked to the clearing and I set up a Mayan-style altar. I included a statue of Ix Chel—the Mayan mother goddess of Earth and moon, along with various images of Mayan gods, including Lord Pacal, who was a powerful ruler of Palenque. I wanted to honor and thank him for the gift of the Maya medicine we would be taking that night.

I began the ceremony by saying a prayer in Mayan, asking permission to open the directions. I opened the portals with prayers, and I asked that we receive protection and guidance during our journey on the medicine. During the ceremony we heard owls hooting around us, which lent a mystical air to the event.

We lit a fire and I offered it a beautiful bundle of black copal incense wrapped in banana leaves that I'd received from my shaman teacher in the Yucatan the year before. The offering was for the healing of Mother Earth. Leif and I took turns saying a prayer of intention for her healing. It was a small, sweet fire and we sat by it till only the embers were left.

We went to our sleeping bags and began to eat the mushrooms. Because of the nausea I had experienced the previous month, we decided to skip lunch and dinner and simply eat the dried mushrooms rather than do a tea. This worked much better and we were so hungry the mushrooms actually tasted pretty good.

We climbed into our sleeping bags and waited for the medicine to take hold. I loved that when I looked up I was looking into a starry sky beyond the treetops. It was magical to be engaging this medicine in the middle of the forest, with no cars whizzing by, no house lights disturbing the dark, just the quiet of the woods and the twinkling of stars above.

I must have drifted off, because when I came to I was feeling very altered. The medicine spoke to me and I could feel its presence around my second chakra. It said, "We're going to work on this area tonight." I acquiesced agreeably, not realizing what I was in for.

Shortly thereafter, I was aware of energetic waves making their way from my genital area up through the center of my body to my throat. It was very pleasurable and as each wave passed through my body, my stomach would contract inward and my torso would quake.

A number of years ago I had a *kundalini* awakening in the Arizona desert, and for a year afterward, every time I lay down to sleep, my body would quake for several minutes. At some point it simply stopped happening.

I was familiar with this energetic sensation in my body but I had never felt it to the degree that I was feeling it now. It began to increase in intensity and my breathing began to quicken. I realized I was making soft moaning sounds and I became very concerned and embarrassed, worrying what Leif would think of me. I didn't want to disturb his journey but I couldn't turn the energy off; it was actually accelerating.

It built to a point of such intensity that my entire body was pulsating with energy. With each wave my back arched and I began to experience full-body orgasms. At one point I said out loud, "What the hell is happening to me?"

The waves kept coming, moving through me relentlessly. By now I was out of my sleeping bag. I'd peeled off my silk long johns and sweater and I was drenched in sweat. Every cell in my body was filled with energy and the full-body pleasure I was experiencing was beyond intense.

Leif told me later that he opened his eyes to see what the hell was going on. He saw me in my white dress with luminous blue light coming off me shooting outward. He said I looked like an angel in the dark. He felt I was bringing through a healing for the Earth. Kundalini energy is highly potent, powerful stuff. In this culture we are not taught how to use sexual energy with consciousness. Something wondrous was clearly moving through me. The triggering of my kundalini certainly upped the ante in terms of the level of vibration my body was sending outward.

At some point the energy lessened and I found myself sitting on my knees, eyes open, looking up at the treetops. I could see different woodland spirits hovering there. I felt a feminine Earth spirit enter my body from beneath the ground. My whole body shifted energetically to accommodate her.

She began directing various spirits to enter my body. At one point the mountain lion came in and my hands went to the ground as I felt the big cat take over my body. The feeling was like an energetic bonding with the essence of the lion. It was as if the lion spirit was exploring the sensation of being in my body as much as I was exploring the sensation of being the lion. It was a meeting of two beings who wished to know each other.

None of the woodland spirits stayed in my body. They would take turns coming in. directed by the main female Earth spirit. She felt authoritative and almost regal. She felt confident to me but she would have no concept of feeling confident. She knew herself no other way. There was no negative, societal conditioning in her—she wasn't human. It was so interesting to feel her. As she stayed with me, I viewed her as a type of guardian around Leif and me. In fact, she loved him fiercely. That was the other piece. Leif is a steward to his land and the forest spirits conveyed to me their deep love and appreciation for him. It was their desire that I let him know that.

When a shaman goes into an ecstatic trance state, she very often returns with messages and guidance for others in the community. The spirits commune with the shaman and give her information for healing, problem solving, and more.

I definitely felt I was being welcomed and engaged by these nature spirits. I also felt an interest on their part in my relationship with Leif. I was sensing a benevolent, conspiratorial energy around bringing us together. I wondered if that was Pan working his magic.

I continued to engage the spirits for quite some time. Then I felt the energetic waves begin to pulsate through my body again, but it was much less intense. All of my senses were heightened and I was attuned to the intelligence of the forest. I could feel the beings around us. I could sense the presence of the fairy realm. I was operating on a whole different level of awareness and it was sublime.

Toward the end of the journey, I reached out in the darkness for Leif's hand, calling his name. I couldn't see a thing but when I felt his hand in mine I almost cried with gratitude for the reconnection with him. I felt like I'd lost all sense of time. When our hands held each other it felt like a uniting of twin energies. I kissed his hand and said, "I love this hand. This is my wing, my beautiful wing. You are my other wing."

Leif told me that as he was lying down waiting for the medicine to take hold, he had his eyes open. He watched in awe as the owl we'd seen earlier flew right over us. We talked for a while longer and then snuggled together, falling asleep in his beautiful woods.

When morning came, we made our way back to the house to our respective beds to sleep in earnest. I awoke midday to brilliant, warm sunshine. I made us a delicious breakfast that we savored. One of the pleasures we shared was food. Leif was not much of a cook, but he understood what real food was and he was an enthusiastic student. Over the course of the next few months, I would teach him how to make traditional healing foods like bone broth and sauerkraut. I also showed him how to roast a chicken and make himself some basic meals that would be nourishing and delicious. To my delight, he began to cook for himself.

We spent the rest of the day soaking up the sun and walking through the enchanted forest that surrounded his home. That night we soaked in the hot tub and retired to our rooms for a deep sleep.

I awoke around four a.m. with Leif's dog curled up with me on the bed. I thought about Leif, asleep in the room next to me. He had held me the night before, when the medicine had subsided. He was once again respectful and sweet. He'd nuzzled in close and I lay with him under the stars in a state of bliss. Thinking of that spurred my desire to reach out to him intimately. I lay in bed going over in my head all the reasons why I shouldn't, until I made a decision that I will never regret. I got out of bed and tiptoed to his bedroom door and peeked inside.

I whispered, "Leif? Are you awake?"

"Yes, darlin'. Are you okay?"

"Would it be all right if I got into bed with you?" And to my relief and delight he answered, "Of course," and moved over to accommodate me. The rest of the weekend was a reverie of soul-nourishing connection.

Reluctantly I left his home, bursting with that uncontainable excitement and joy that comes when one has fallen in love. The friendship was already there, and we had a solid bond of mutual trust. I was grateful for the opportunity to connect so meaningfully with him as he was a genuinely beautiful person.

The medicine journey I'd experienced had also been deeply meaningful and unexpected. Not only had it reawakened my kundalini, it connected me to the nature spirits in a very unusual way. I hadn't heard of people bringing through spirits on the medicine. I was very curious about just what was possible with the use of the mushrooms. I imagined the medicine experiences would be directly relational to the individual makeup of each person who partook. I was blown away by what was possible and shocked by this sudden turn of events in my life. It was a wild and uncharted path on so many levels, and one I decided to fearlessly walk.

≈ 7 ≈

Deception

To relationship we bring so much hope, so much need, and so much capacity for disappointment. Anyone who looks back from midlife must shudder at the enormity of such choices as marriage and career often made decades before, and the unconsciousness out of which they were made. Young people have always fallen in love, promised life-long commitment and made babies. They will continue to do so. But during the Middle Passage many will confront themselves and their partners, putting enormous strain on the relationship. Indeed, there are few midlife marriages, if they have survived, that are not under great strain. Either divorce is the signal event which launches the Middle Passage, or the marriage becomes a prime focus for those tectonic pressures.

—James Holliss, The Middle Passage: From Misery to Meaning in Midlife

I returned home a married woman deeply in love with another man. Although Richard and I were clearly over, nothing had been formally discussed. Our therapy sessions were teaching me a great deal about our roles in the marriage, but of course they were not actually helping our relationship. I wasn't present to the marriage any longer. It was not fair to Richard, but I was feeling paralyzed with fear about how to end it.

There was no money to leave and get a place with my girls. At the same time, my teaching was beginning to take off and I knew it would be my livelihood soon, but not soon enough. I could judge myself and choose to spiral down a labyrinth of self-hatred, but I felt strangely right about everything—even being in the tension of marital discord and deception.

It was not lost on me that I was now in a similar position as Richard's ex-wife. She too, fell in love with another man and eventually left Richard. I was now learning about my own judgment and the importance of compassion.

I'd felt morally superior to that woman and I never once took the time to wonder what she was going through. Until we've walked in someone else's shoes, we really don't have a right to judge. And what is judgment? Often it is a casting out of the very aspects of ourselves that we don't or won't carry. We project them onto another, usually with a healthy dose of self-righteous indignation. So, I had to withdraw not only my judgment of Richard's ex-wife, but also judgment of myself. And I had to come into compassion for the two of us.

Several months ago, Richard had had his chart done and was told he was entering a Pluto transit which would last for three years. This was a once-in-a-280-year cycle that most of us never experience. Pluto is the annihilator and it will obliterate any belief systems you have about yourself and your world. Richard was told he would be a completely different person at the end of the transit and that everything in his life would change as a result. The astrologer joked with Richard, asking how strong his marriage was. I remember listening and knowing in my heart that I would play a major role in his Pluto transit, and it wouldn't be fun.

Interestingly, my astrological chart showed that I was in the last year of a thirty-year cycle, meaning I was in a period of endings. The whole thing felt almost scripted. I was in a dissolving state. Even the plant medicine was dissolving me on levels I couldn't imagine.

I knew that Richard was also done with the marriage but had not admitted it to himself. He hadn't mentioned a word to anyone that the marriage was falling apart. He never fought to keep me either. He seemed resigned about the whole thing. I was certain he was more concerned with how another failed marriage would make him look. I was not concerned about that for myself. I had long stopped dancing to the eyes of others and I frankly didn't give a farthing what people thought of me. My close friends knew me and loved me and that was enough.

I thought about how this impending divorce would affect my girls. They adored Richard. He was a playful, loving stepfather. A split between Richard and me would be no surprise to them, as they had seen me sleep in the guest room many times during past disagreements. I did not want to model a loveless marriage for my girls. At the same time, I was terrified about going out on my own as a single mother. I received child support from their dad, but it would not be enough to cover monthly expenses.

I would have to call upon all my resourcefulness. I knew I could make a living as a spiritual teacher. The women who worked with me were experiencing great personal shifts. Word about my classes and monthly ceremonies was continuing to spread. There had been so much interest in my medicine-wheel training that I had to put together a second group. I knew if I kept working at what I loved, I would be supported. It would require a leap of faith in Spirit and absolute trust in myself.

In terms of my burgeoning relationship with Leif, I was being supported in the most surprising ways. I'd been without a car for over a year. My car had died and Richard would not take out a loan for a new one. He preferred I use his car and figured we'd buy one when his business turned around. It was a three-and-a-half-hour drive to Leif's house and I happened to have a friend who had three cars. She made a car available every time I wanted to visit Leif. It was amazing.

My ex-husband took our girls regularly so I was always able to schedule my visits to Leif when my girls were with their father. It was win-win. I could spend time with Leif, and my girls had time with their dad. I would return to them happy, nurtured, and hopeful for the future.

The eventual ending of my marriage would ultimately serve Richard as well. No doubt he would find someone new, hopefully someone better suited to his personality. We were so different as people. We'd had a strong spiritual connection for the first few years and that was wonderful. Eventually, we each took a different direction on our respective spiritual paths. That might not pose a problem for some, but Richard and I had very different philosophies on a number of issues that were important to us. That, coupled with the extremely difficult years with his daughter, created a vast chasm between us that never healed.

I am profoundly grateful to him for creating the platform for my unfolding as a spiritual teacher. Very few men would have understood that desire in a partner. On that level, Richard had always supported me. I know there were times he felt jealous as he watched me step into my role as teacher. Teaching was something he also felt called to, but his business demanded his full attention.

Divorce is never fun. There are many different expressions of it, but most are emotionally taxing. I knew I was entering a whole new phase of my life. I chose to move forward with as much courage and grace as I could muster.

≈ 8 ≈

Six Grams and a Grandmother's Scolding

*The mushrooms, which grow only during the season of tor-
rential rains, awaken the forces of creation and produce an
experience of spiritual abundance, of an astonishing, inex-
haustible constitution of forms that identifies them with fertility and makes them a mediation, a means of communion,
of communication between man and the natural world of
which they are the metaphysical flesh.*
                    —Henry Munn, *The Mushrooms of Language*
From *Hallucinogens & Shamanism*, Michael J. Harner, ed.

For our third immersion in the medicine together, we
worked again with the Palenque mushrooms. After
experiencing full-body kundalini energetics, I was more
than a little eager to try them out again.

Leif and I discussed dosage, as we found these mushrooms to be milder than the first strain we used. We made
a decision to do six grams each. We also decided to shift
our ceremonial space to just inside the grove of trees that
carried a beautiful energy.

On the other side was a small open grove with a large tree in the corner. The tree had lots of crevices around its base that looked like little altar spaces. There were other smaller trees around the edges of the grove, giving the space a sense of protection and privacy. It was a perfect spot for our ceremony.

I brought another crystal offering for the trees. I also brought a pair of dragonflies as offerings. They would fly around my garden in the summer and every so often, one would get caught in the house. If I saw one, I would catch it and release it outside.

A few weeks earlier, I'd found a dead dragonfly sitting on my front hall carpet. It was a wonder it was still there as I had two cats and two daughters, all of whom would have loved to find it. I picked it up and put it on my altar.

The dragonfly feels very fairy-like and it occurred to me that it would be lovely to place a pair of them within the grove of trees on Leif's land as an offering to the nature spirits. I saw them as representing our respective connections to the nature realms. I only had one so far, so I asked the deva of the dragonfly if it would gift me with one more for Leif.

A few days before I was to leave for my weekend, I found a dying dragonfly on my hallway carpet. I took it outside and placed it in the shade to see if it would recover. Instead, it slowly and quietly died, leaving me its body to gift to our sacred grove.

Before we started our ceremony, we both climbed up to the little cluster of trees and made our offering. I also gifted my crystal. I was going to do another Mayan-style ceremony in honor of our Palenque mushrooms. It had been raining earlier so we opted out of doing fire. Leif tied a tarp overhang to the trees framing our grove so we'd be protected from the rain. We set up our sleeping bags and blankets and proceeded with the ceremony. Then we sat down across from each other and each ate six grams of mushrooms. Settling into our sleeping bags, we waited for our journeys to begin.

My journey began with the woods crying their tears through me. Builders were raping the land around us. The whole of my being was consumed with the sorrow and anguish of the forest. I gave myself up to it and felt it move through my body to express its pain. At one point I heard myself saying out loud, "I weep the woods!" I felt a flooding of desperation, sadness, disbelief, and pain. It was so much to bear. It broke my heart.

Later I moved to a completely different state of being as I felt the waves of energy moving up my body once again. This time I was being made love to by the Earth. It was intoxicating and incredibly pleasurable. My whole body was moving with energy as I whispered, "Sweet mama. Sweet mama." I was in a state of ecstatic bliss as waves from the Earth beneath me filled my body and triggered my kundalini.

The journey was so multi-layered it is hard to keep track of it all. I saw myself at one point taken down into the womb of Mother Earth. She made a place for me to sit down and called me her "gentle daughter." Gentle is not a word that anyone has used to describe me. Then I understood that spirits see with razor acuity far beyond our masks and personas and straight into the essence of our being. The Earth Goddess saw the essence of my heart and that was a profound healing for me.

Then the fairies came into me and I heard a laughter coming from myself that I'd never heard before; it was otherworldly. I felt pure delight and joy as we explored each other in this most unusual way.

I would go from one experience to another and at times simply drift into such a deep state I lost consciousness. The medicine was feeling much more powerful than it had the previous month.

As I moved to another state of being I heard an owl calling, and I "felt" its call. I responded with sounds that were completely unfamiliar but they came out of my mouth as fluently as any foreign language. I waited and the owl called back. I responded again in the same way and waited. Again, the owl called. I responded one more time and waited, but there was silence.

After that I felt myself flying over a Taoist monastery. I knew in that moment that Leif and I had lived there in another lifetime during which we'd been dear old friends, like brothers. I felt the monks sending up their blessings to Leif and me in this life. I was surprised to see that they knew I was hovering above them. I saw three sets of three Taoist glyphs lifting upward toward me. They were sending blessings to us. It was very beautiful.

At one point I checked in with Leif, who patiently informed me that he was communing with the moss and would be with me shortly. I responded, "Okay. I will wait."

A moment later I was swept downward to the realm of the slugs and snails. This was a very peaceful, gentle space. Leif is particularly drawn to the mollusks and it was quite something to experience their world. They held a very soft, calm energy, and my whole being dropped into a slow, gentle vibration while in their presence.

Eventually, Leif and I connected, but we were still very deep in the medicine. I was experiencing sporadic, full-body kundalini waves and I was laughing in pleasure. At that moment Leif felt a slug on his hand. He was delighted and asked if he could put it on me.

"Sure," I replied, and he placed it on my neck. As soon as he put it there my entire body was rocked with energy, but it was coming from this tiny creature! It was the strangest, most incredible sensation. It built to a crescendo and I had another full-body orgasm. I was incredulous and then I cried, "I think I've had a slug-gasm!" This was the funniest thing I'd ever heard and we broke into riotous laughter. We were now officially in the realms of the ridiculous.

It then occurred to me to repeat the entire version of Gilbert and Sullivan's "Modern Major General" that I had memorized in a moment of inspiration. I had recited it to him earlier that day and he was very impressed. Now I was going to do so on six grams of psilocybin.

As I recited the first stanza, Leif burst out laughing.

"I am the very model of a modern major general
I've information vegetable, animal and mineral
I know the kings of England and I quote the fights historical
From Marathon to Waterloo, in order categorical.
I'm very well acquainted, too, with matters mathematical
I understand equations, both the simple and quadratical.
About binomial theorem I am teeming with a lot o' news
With many cheerful facts about the square of the hypotenuse."

We were screaming with laughter and when I had finished all six stanzas I said, "Well, I figured if you were on the fence about whether you loved me or not, this would clinch it!"

"Well, I wasn't really sure, but I am now!" Leif responded.

To which I replied, "Well GOOD, 'cause that's IT, babe! That's all I got! I'm out of tricks after this one!"

We laughed like two old friends and I felt the Earth laughing with us. Laughter is the best medicine and that night I felt the part of me that resists joy and playfulness simply dissolve away.

And I think I can say with certainty that "Modern Major General" has never been recited on six grams of psilocybin before, nor will it likely happen ever again.

After our mutual exploration into the ridiculous, we both fell back into our respective journeys. I was getting tired but my body was pulsating with the medicine. It felt like I'd drunk ten cups of coffee. I could feel my nervous system starting to fry. All of a sudden, a grandmother appeared to me looking very concerned and said, "Daughter, you are doing good work. But this is too much medicine. You must not do this much again." I nodded and told her I would be more careful.

As I lay in discomfort, five grandmothers floated in who called themselves the "whispering grandmothers." They floated around me and in me, and I understood that they were calming my nervous system so I could unwind and sleep. I could hear whispers—it was a very soft, gentle sensation, and it lulled me into a calm state.

I loved these medicine journeys. They offered me direct engagement with strange and exquisite spirits. I was very humbled to have the grandmothers come to me. I worked with them closely in my shamanic work and sang them through with a crystal-singing bowl. To have them engage me on the medicine made me feel supported and loved.

Leif and I eventually made our way back to the house for another delicious breakfast. We poured ourselves into bed and sank into a deep sleep. There was a great sense of mirth to the remainder of our weekend together. I had a feeling that through this last medicine journey, I'd cleared a block that was keeping me from expressing my playful side. Spirits are often known for their sense of humor and I wondered if they were possibly working on me through the medicine, giving me an assist to connect to my joy. It had been a long time since I'd felt that kind of levity. I had a sense that the mushrooms were peeling away layers of old belief patterns and conditioning. I was intrigued, and I made a decision to continue with my in-depth explorations of this extraordinary magical medicine.

❧ 9 ❧

Initiating the End

Ruin is a gift. Ruin is the road to transformation.
  —Elizabeth Gilbert, *Eat Pray Love*

Coming home from that weekend, I felt unburdened of the depression I'd carried for the last few years. During the height of difficulty with Claire and Richard, I was so consumed with my own frustration and powerlessness I could barely smile. A good friend at the time had said to me, "Sweetie, you're not fun anymore. You used to be so funny, but you've lost your joy."

That night on the medicine, I released the part of me that I'd repressed these past few years. I had been so trapped in my perceived helplessness that I'd forgotten how to feel levity. I had my sense of it now and I was viewing my life with much more optimism. Even my daughters noticed the change in me, saying, "Mom, you're so *happy!*"

My living situation at home was tolerable, but I was not in alignment with the truth of where I was with regard to Richard. Leif was a catalyst for ending this marriage, although the fact is that it had been over for at least two years. I was too afraid of how I would support my girls and myself to actually end the marriage any sooner. Now, I could no longer be in my marriage—it was over. For the past four years my girls had witnessed Richard and me in conflict. Our latest row had lasted over a month. The fact that my girls were so surprised to see me *happy* really hit home.

I wanted my daughters to know me as someone who lived in her truth, even if it meant going against what others thought was right. I already had a couple of friends asking, "What about your girls? How are you going to support them? Why don't you hang on until they've graduated high school?" I could feel these women projecting their fears onto me. This is a common conundrum for women, even today. Here I was, pushing fifty, with no firmly established career and no steady paycheck, about to end my marriage and leave a big, beautiful home on five acres in lovely Redmond, Washington. I was going to leave a man who was a good provider and a basic all-round good guy. I'm sure to the average observer I appeared to be out of my mind.

Here is what I understood. I had been desperately unhappy and lonely in my marriage. I had come to a place where I knew it had to end, and at the same time, I knew that it was imperative for me to own my part in what we'd created, good and not so good. I could leave the marriage as victim and tell my sad tale of woe for the rest of my life, or I could take this as an opportunity to look deeply into myself and make some major changes in the way I approached relationship.

This was also an opportune time to come into my power. I had always had a man support me financially. There were times I had brought in some money, but the areas I was drawn to were always more creative and they did not pay very well.

Now I was teaching fairly regularly. I had an exciting tour coming up in a year that I would be leading in the Yucatan and I would be paid for that. I was beginning to see that I was at a place in my life where I could do what I loved AND make it my livelihood. I would have to really work at it, but I carried an inner taskmaster and was no stranger to self-discipline.

I decided to initiate ending our marriage in the presence of our therapist so that if Richard went into reaction or denial, she would be there to mediate and assist us. As it turned out, that day was a full moon in the sign of Aries. Aries is the great inciter and when I read about the energies of that moon it said, "A focus on the Self and initiating something bold and courageous will be the order of the day." I took that as a sign that the forces were with me and plunged ahead.

We began our session and I was asked to share first. I faced Richard, and from a heartfelt place I told him that our marriage was over. It was an emotional hour for both of us. I think Richard was in shock, as he was very good at putting on blinders and often the obvious would escape his awareness altogether. When we got into the car after the hour of discussion around ending the marriage, he asked me again if that was indeed what we were doing. Rather than the usual irritation I would have felt in the past for such a question, I felt a wave of compassion for him as I watched him struggle with the realization that our marriage was over.

It was my hope that we would endeavor to end our marriage with as much consciousness as we possibly could. We'd both done a great deal of psycho-spiritual work, and a life transition like this was where the rubber meets the road. We could devolve into anger, blame, and victim, or we could act with maturity and acceptance. I knew we'd have our moments—we were human after all. I also recognized it would not be an ugly process.

We had a chance to end our marriage with dignity and asked our therapist to recommend a divorce attorney who wasn't an asshole. We worked with a firm called Peaceful Separations. There was no money for fancy lawyers and this firm allowed us to download a form and do most of the work on our own. If we could not be civil and fair with each other, this would be a nightmare. In a way it was a test. What better medium to assess your spiritual evolution than divorce?

In terms of my girls, who were now eleven and almost fourteen, I was very upfront with them about the breakup. They loved Richard and he loved them. He was a wonderful stepdad and I assured them that they would always have access to him. My girls took it very well. Of course, they were still living in our home so they had not yet experienced the uprooting and the adjustment they would have to make to a smaller, more modest home. All of that they could handle, though. I just didn't want them to endure an ugly divorce, and both Richard and I were very conscious of that.

Needless to say, Richard was experiencing his own feelings around the failure of the marriage. We weren't talking much other than during our therapy sessions. Thankfully, though, there were no angry words. It was obvious this chapter in our lives was closing and we just had to hang in there until we could make the changes we both desired in our living arrangements.

There are thousands of couples in this country who are now separated or divorced and still sharing a home. We were blessed to live in a large rambler so there was plenty of space for both of us. The fact that we didn't despise each other was also a huge gift. This would continue to be home to both of us until the divorce was finalized and I was ready to move out.

It would take us another couple of months to actually sit down and go over the divorce forms, but the energy of endings had been set in motion. I was nervous about the future and at the same time, greatly relieved.

⇌ 10 ⇋

Love and Death on Liberty Caps

*In knowing Self, we transcend our identity. The death of
identity is the birth into the knowing of Self.*
—Michael J. Roads, *Through the Eyes of Love, Book II*

The next medicine journey with Leif was going to be
with locally grown wild mushrooms that he'd picked
near his home. The Liberty Caps grew prolifically in various areas of Washington and because they grew wild, they
were exposed to the sun, the moon, and all the elements.
There is a different quality to wild-grown medicine and I
was looking forward to the experience.

Sitting in Leif's kitchen, he told me that the Liberty
Caps were an extremely potent strain of mushroom. I
looked at the tiny dried mushrooms inside the glass jar
and they resembled daddy longlegs spiders. The stem was
wispy, thread-like, with the tiniest little head at the end.
They looked benign enough, but what did I know?

We walked out to our ceremony space in the woods
to set up for the evening. It was the end of October, so we
would have to bundle up in order to stay outside the whole
night. This time Leif was going to lead us in ceremony

before we took the medicine. I loved his sensitivity around the creatures of nature. I had seen him stop to gently lift up a slug and place it away from the footpath. He was like an elemental, and I knew his ceremony would be heartfelt and deep.

When darkness came, we were standing in our sacred grove. Leif lit a candle and began the ceremony. Unlike my ceremonies where I spoke throughout, Leif's ceremony was silent and humble and beautifully reverent. I am a talker and no slouch at expressing myself. Leif possesses the ability to convey deep feeling through silence. To people with sensitivity, this quiet depth of expression can be felt more profoundly than any flowery words of poetic prose. I was in the presence of a humble master. I felt indescribable gratitude for the privilege of engaging this medicine in such richly beautiful surroundings with a man of gentleness, strength, and humility. He was a fierce old warrior but he was also a gentle healer. I was proud to have him as my friend and my love.

We sat down and ate our wispy, spidery mushrooms. Never judge a book by its cover—not ever! Those wimpy shreds of air-like fungus created the most powerful, intense journey I had yet to experience.

The medicine came on very intensely, taking me by surprise. I had been fighting a urinary tract infection earlier in the week and I was lamenting the sensation of it as I was lying down. I saw elves working on my lower belly and they told me they would take care of it for me, which they did.

I felt myself under the Earth and I was talking to the mushroom people. At the same time I felt Leif's presence around me telling me to just "let go." I had a sense of him as a kind of spirit guide and I was enjoying the feeling of having him with me on this journey. At one point the mushrooms acknowledged that

I was thinking of him. I felt my whole being smile. The mushrooms seemed pleased and said, "You are heart-bound." I loved that and said, "Yes! I am!"

Then they said the strangest thing. "We brought you together." All I could say, which was sincere, was, "Thank you."

And then they said, "You are betrothed."

How strange that they would say that. A few weeks before, Leif and I had attended a workshop given by a spiritual teacher. On the ferry coming home, just before it docked and a good-bye was imminent, I had removed one of five golden bamboo rings I wore and placed it on his right ring finger. I did it without even thinking: it was an act of the heart. Leif took it a step further, removing it and putting it on his left ring finger. It was a sweet, romantic moment.

I knew that with each ceremony we created in that beautiful grove, we were cementing a bond of love and trust that ran deeper than perhaps we even knew. In these magical realms, I felt we were indeed betrothed.

After my conversation with the mushrooms, I asked to see the fairies. Immediately, I felt them come into me and I experienced a rush of joy and delight. Again, the laughter came through me, sounding not like my laughter at all. It was light and kind of high-pitched and almost musical. Having that energy move through me felt wondrous. I was connected to an energy that was totally clear in its expression of joy and delight.

At one point, the mountain lion came in and I climbed partly out of my sleeping bag, turning over with my hands on the ground like a cat. I had come to expect its presence with each medicine journey. It had thus far never spoken to me. It seemed to want to possess me momentarily where we could both experience exploring the essence of each other.

The mushrooms were increasing in intensity and I felt myself slipping deeper into an Alice in Wonderland rabbit hole.

Sometime later, I came to consciousness only to discover that I could not feel my body. I had no sense of it anymore; I was actually part of the Earth. The moon was almost full and I was looking into the area just outside our grove of trees that was bathed in moonlight. There was a tiny tree next to me with leaves on it that glowed softly. I was in a state of complete calm and . . . I thought I was dead. My sense was that I was in the between world after death. Not embodied, but not in "heaven" either.

I called softly to Leif but he didn't answer. Unbeknownst to me, he had gone off in the woods to pee and had a hell of a time finding his way back. He, too, was deep into the medicine.

I lay there truly thinking that I was dead and trying to remember what my life had been. I was stripped of all memory other than I knew I was with Leif.

I must have slipped into unconsciousness because when I came to again, I called for Leif and he said, "I'm right here, darlin'. I couldn't find you but I finally made my way back to you."

We began a dialogue that was almost a comedy of errors but it was not humorous. In my mind, I thought we were in the world between lifetimes and this was our sacred grove that we would return to after each life to reunite. He just thought we were having a conversation, so there was a developing miscommunication that made things very interesting.

When he said he couldn't find me but he found his way back to me, I thought he was returning from a lifetime where we didn't find each other. I was thinking that we would come and go from this grove as we went to experience different lives and sometimes we would find each other and other times we would not. I really thought this was so.

Then Leif began talking about ranger buddies of his that he saw on his medicine journey but to my mind, I thought he was telling me of his most recent lifetime.

At some point I asked him, "Why do we keep doing this?" What I meant was, why do we keep living these lives over and over? But of course, I didn't convey it that way and Leif thought I was talking about the mushrooms.

He said something like, "It's good for us! It's what we do!"

"But we forget who we are! I don't want to forget anymore! I don't want to do this anymore!"

I meant living lifetime after lifetime and going into forgetting, but Leif responded with, "Darlin', we're right on schedule. It will be over before you know it." He was talking about the medicine wearing off in a couple of hours.

I thought he meant that we wouldn't have to keep incarnating much longer. Being right on schedule told me he knew something I didn't about when the incarnations were going to end.

Whenever I would softly call to him, he would answer me with such love. He would say, "I'm right here, my love. I love you."

I was beginning to think that he was a god who I returned to after each lifetime and he would welcome me back with loving words. He certainly spoke to me with the kind of love I would imagine a god would have for me.

It was so, so strange. My lifetime as Shonagh was gone, other than I knew my name and I knew Leif's name. At one point I asked him, "Who are you?"

"I'm your Leif, my love."

All that did was convince me that he was some kind of a welcoming god to me.

Then he asked, "How was your journey, my love?"

Again, I thought he was asking me about my last lifetime and I said, "I can't remember. I can't remember anything."

Then I asked him, "Who am I?"

To which he replied laughing, "You're my Shonagh."

That made me think that maybe I was some kind of an Earth goddess who returns to the Earth after each lifetime. I was racking my brain to see if there was some goddess named Shonagh that I was supposed to know about.

Finally I remembered my girls. I started to panic because I realized I couldn't remember how my life with them had ended. I became distraught and asked, "Leif, where are my girls? What happened to them?"

I was wanting to know what life they were in now and what had happened, but Leif, who by now was getting a little worried about me, said, "Babe, they're with their dad this weekend. They're just fine. They're having a great time."

Then I remembered Richard and I asked worriedly about him. "What happened to Richard? Was he okay?"

"Richard is just fine, babe." Then Leif thought that maybe I wanted to go back to the house and get out of the forest and he said, "We can go back to the house if you want. We can go back and drink broth and sit in the kitchen for awhile."

That totally confused me. I thought of Leif's sweet house where I felt so happy. It felt like a kind of heaven that we would go to between lives. I thought he was saying we would go there soon. I was still not feeling my body. In my mind I was still part of the Earth, so I wasn't sure how I was going to get to his house with no body. At the same time, I longed to be there and feel "normal" so I could enjoy myself.

It was the most bizarre, strange experience. I had been completely stripped of my identity and was not a human anymore, but a spirit that was part of the Earth. My only reference point was Leif and even then, I wasn't entirely sure exactly what or who he was. I just knew we were connected in love and this was our in-between place.

I was not happy, though. I wanted to remember. I wanted the lifetimes to stop, as the thought of going into forgetting again made me sad. I wanted to stay in the love.

I wonder now if there is sadness on a soul's part when it has to leave its space of light and beauty to incarnate as a human. I would imagine there are some souls who aren't exactly chomping at the bit to come here and forget themselves and their connection to Love.

At some point I was finally able to move and I reached out once again for his hand, which I kissed repeatedly. We were going to try to sleep but I was genuinely afraid to do so.

Then Leif walked off to pee and I was on my knees weeping. He came back and asked, "Are you crying? Darlin', why are you crying?"

"I'm afraid to go to sleep. Who will I be when I wake up?"

He hugged me while I cried and said, "You'll be my beautiful Shonagh. It's okay. You'll be okay, babe."

That was the deepest, most mysterious and profound medicine journey yet. I would need time to integrate what happened to me. It was as if a bomb went off in my psyche and my whole self as I knew her was obliterated. "Shonagh" was gone. No memory of her life. No body. "I" was simply "awareness" living in the Earth. All the layers of myself had dissolved until there was no "me" left.

Through the medicine I had experienced a shamanic "death," only to see that there is no death. It is said that shamans are not afraid to die because they have already died. Shamanism is not a belief system; it is a system of knowledge that is directly experienced first-hand by the senses. Having a direct experience of this profundity was a sacred gift. I do not underestimate the power of plant medicine to carry us into states of awareness that rock the very foundation of our being.

In the dissolving of my identity, I experienced myself beyond the confines of my perception of who I thought

I was. This was both scary and exciting for me. I always understood intellectually that I was self and Self. Now I had direct experience of myself beyond my identity. The "Shonagh" I knew in this lifetime was an identity made up of a series of constructs. They formed the idea of who I thought I was, but it wasn't the whole story, not even close.

In the "death" state on the medicine, "I" was present, but there was no identification with any of the constructs that had created the identity of Shonagh. I just was. The only thing I recognized was Love. I connected to Leif and felt his love for me, and that was all I wanted. In that state, I had no desire to go back into "forgetting" and the loss of connection to Love.

In his book, *Mushrooms and Mankind: The Impact of Mushrooms on Human Consciousness and Religion,* James Arthur says, "The nature of the hero's journey towards immortality is also associated with the search for an ultimate truth, and finding it is a necessary step toward this goal of immortality. This also is a step taken in shamanism, which the plant entheogens are known to teach, if one is able to understand.

"It is this teaching which must strip away that which is in conflict with the natural indigenous makeup of the individual seeker's belief system. Tuning the mind towards the higher frequency vibrations must be accomplished in order to conquer death on a spiritual (which is also a physical) level. When the physical body dies, the spirit is thought to wake—but only if the hero is able to make this happen. This is the practice of shamanism, the journey into the death experience, and the deep psychological introspection/judgment through plant-induced states in preparation for the inevitability of the ultimate event, the crowning glory of life itself—death. This is at the forefront of the shamanic practice rather than a quest relegated to the deity one worships. It resides at the core of individual experience."

Everything society had told me I was had been stripped away during this experience. I was coming closer to true knowing of Self. Veils were lifting for me on this medicine. I knew I was meant to engage this path and I knew the experience would be life transforming. I had actively sought to know myself more deeply. I knew that the path to Self would be the most profound and numinous mystery I could ever hope to explore.

I welcomed the dissolving and opened my heart to the mystery of death and transformation.

⁓ 11 ⁓

Owl Medicine

The owl is a symbol of the feminine, the moon, and the night. To the ancient Greeks, the owl was associated with the goddess Athena and it was a symbol of higher wisdom. It was the guardian of the Acropolis. To the early Christian Gnostics, it is associated with Lilith, the first wife of Adam who refused to be submissive to him. To the Pawnee, it was a symbol of protection. To the Ojibwa, it was a symbol of evil and death. To the Pueblo, it was associated with the Skeleton Man, the god of death, but who was also a spirit of fertility. Owl medicine is symbolically associated with clairvoyance, astral projection and magic, both black and white.
—Ted Andrews, *Animal Speak*

The last medicine journey shook me to my core. My dedicated exploration of the mushroom medicine was bringing me to a place of knowing myself far beyond my cultural conditioning. The experiences on the medicine were giving me a whole new understanding of my connection with everything around me.

Something particularly wondrous began happening that was directly related to the medicine journeys. Leif and I had felt the presence of the owl around us and had come to think of it as a guardian of sorts. During each of our shared medicine journeys, the owl was close by, hooting in the near vicinity. I was feeling owl around me in my daily life and it seemed to be making its presence more apparent each day.

Two years ago I was in the Yucatan working with my shaman teacher. One day he took me to see a Mayan shaman for a blessing ceremony. After it was over, I thanked the shaman and left his home. He came running after me and gifted me with a necklace that held an owl pendant. I remember wondering why an owl. I kept it on my altar, treasuring the gift. I realize now that he could see owl around me before I had any awareness of it.

The owl was coming into my life now in a very pronounced way. In October, I visited a school that my daughters would be applying to, only to discover that their mascot was the owl. Entering the school's library, we were greeted by a striking photo of an owl staring at us from the magazine rack. Everywhere we walked on campus we saw representations of owls. It couldn't have made itself more seen if it tried.

At this time, I began running very early in the morning while it was still dark. On these runs I heard owls calling to each other. I had no idea there were owls living so close by. One night I was awakened around midnight to the hooting of an owl. I thought it was impossible, as the window was shut. I got up to check, and someone had left it open. It hooted again, while I stood at the window, sounding like it was just at the end of the driveway.

After my latest medicine journey with Leif, I received a phone call from a Native American friend who was a gifted artisan of animal medicine pieces. Joseph called to say he'd been thinking about me lately and had something he felt belonged to me. He explained that he'd been saving something he'd found on one of his walks when he was much younger. Joseph felt compelled to give away this special item now. He wanted me to come in person so I could see it. I asked if he could tell me what it was. He hesitated and then said, "It's a handful of feathers from a white owl."

I felt myself go weak. This was too strange. I had tears of emotion running down my cheeks and I told him I would come that week. A few years before this, when I was working with my teacher, Brugh Joy, I shared an experience with him where a white bat hovered in front of my face in the darkness. I'd had my eyes wide open and was face to face with this being. Brugh talked to me about the symbolic nature of the bat and explained that when an animal comes to you and it is white, this is an indication that this is a sacred being. It requires your full attention and has something invaluable to impart.

I made the long drive to see Joseph the day before I was to teach my second medicine-wheel training. I was way too busy for a lengthy round-trip excursion, but when Spirit calls you in this way, you make the time to show up for what is being gifted.

Joseph pulled out a box wrapped in red fabric. He opened it up and removed the feathers from the tissue. They were so beautiful and light. They had a lovely feminine quality to them and I could feel the tears welling up as I ran my fingers over the silky soft feathers. Joseph is a master artisan and he suggested making them into a fan with a beautiful beaded handle. I loved the idea.

Then he told me that he knew of two people who practiced "white owl medicine." One had been a friend who had since passed away, and the other was an eighty-six-year-old Native American man who was one of his teachers. He explained that white owl medicine works with the divine child and it is the protector of children. It heals very deeply but gently. Joseph told me that I would work with this medicine and I would be guided as to how to do so.

I left his home feeling immense gratitude for what was unfolding in my life. I was being guided and gifted beyond anything I could imagine. It was humbling and also very exciting. Owl medicine had come to me and I opened my heart to receive its wisdom.

The following morning I awoke with a dream. I saw myself dressed in white in the center of a circle of people who were also in white. I was waving the owl fan over a woman in the center of the circle, using it to clear her field and infuse her with the medicine. I decided then that I would do a white owl medicine healing for my moon ceremony in January 2012. I felt it would bring a beautiful healing for the women as they embraced the energies of the coming new year.

In the meantime, I began doing a little research into owl medicine. According to Ted Andrews, in his book, *Animal Speak,* "The owl was a symbol of the feminine, the moon, and the dark." I learned that owl medicine enables the practitioner to know what others are hiding. As we well know, owls see clearly in the darkness. This can make people uncomfortable, however, practitioners of owl medicine can plumb depths within another's soul. This can assist with understanding and healing deeper personal material.

Owl medicine is about intuition, wisdom, and the power of the knowing. The Greek goddess of wisdom,

Athena, is shown with an owl on her shoulder. It would light up her blind side, illuminating the truth.

Owl is also seen as a harbinger of death and many native cultures regarded it with fear and superstition. Because it is a creature of the night and moves in silence, they saw the owl as the bringer of black magic and danger.

The owl is a powerful ally for shamans who perform soul retrieval. Its ability to see in the dark provides an assist to the shaman as she traverses the realms of spirit. I practiced soul retrieval in my healing work and made a mental note to begin working with the owl in that capacity.

It was apparent that I was being guided more deeply into the spirit realms and the owl felt like a prominent ally on the path. As the mushroom journeys were about engaging the realms of spirit, I felt I was being gifted with a wise and capable protector and guide.

~ 12 ~

The Succubus

The moon, a day before full,
hung suspended low to the horizon
above the tree line
hauntingly, disquiet settled on us
It wasn't the buck moon this day
No it was a Blood Moon,
a harbinger, a foretaste…
  —Raymond A. Foss, *'Blood Moon'* from *Poetry Where*
You Live

My next medicine journey took place the night before a full-moon eclipse. Leif and I had decided to do this one indoors as it was now mid-December and far too cold to be spending the night in the forest. Neither of us considered the swirling energies of the full-moon eclipse that were already occurring around us. Full moons are a portal that can bring through every conceivable kind of energy. Eclipses are highly impactful on the personal level as well as the collective. Ancient cultures regarded eclipses with fear and respect, for they understood that great and long-lasting change occurred as a result.

We decided to combine mushroom strains and mixed three grams of cyanescens with two grams of the Liberty Caps. Both strains grow prolifically in the Pacific Northwest. We set up an area in the living room where we would be lying down for the journey. Leif smudged and we proceeded to take the medicine.

As my digestion is sometimes slow, the medicine took a longer time than normal to take hold. I began to think this was a mild dose, which proved to be far from true.

My journey eventually began with the face of an owl, its eyes penetrating me. After it disappeared I felt the presence of the grandmothers around me. At that same time, the mountain lion came in. I had decided earlier that I would engage this spirit in conversation. It showed up on every journey. It would come into me but I had never had an actual conversation with it.

It felt my desire and said, "Let us stalk your marriage, and find all the moments when you strayed from the beauty way." I understood this to mean that more shadow work was necessary and I began in earnest. The grandmothers then told me that each example I found would be a piece of kindling that I would burn in a fire when I was done. I proceeded to observe myself at times, exerting my control, casting judgment, and withholding compassion. It was going to be a large fire. The final piece was my rage, and when that was added to the pile, it went up in a great blaze of flames.

Then the grandmothers said, "Now you can sit in the circle, daughter. You are clear." I felt a sense of joy and levity. They called me in to the experience more deeply by saying, "Feel us, daughter." I let myself be bathed in a sea of love.

At that moment, Leif began talking about the devastation the Earth is enduring at the hands of man. He expressed his pain and frustration with a world that dishonors nature in the most deplorable ways.

I went inside the Earth to speak with her about it. She told me very matter-of-factly that she would be swallowing up many areas. Her reply was delivered without malice. It was simply her response and I did not for one moment doubt her intent. I believe these are the Earth changes that every indigenous culture has predicted, and I think we are in for a wild ride in the near future.

Awhile after that, I found myself sitting again with the grandmothers, who told me that I "dance the dance of the good daughter." I took this to mean that they were acknowledging the work I was doing, being in service at this time in my life.

Next I found myself crying to Leif. I was seeing him as some kind of god or father figure, and I was telling him that I dance the dance of the good daughter for him. I asked him to please not leave me.

Leif responded, telling me that he loved me and he wasn't going anywhere.

When I engage these deep shamanic states, I realize I am cracking open the deep recesses of my psyche. Somewhere in me is an aspect of my soul that needs to be acknowledged as "good enough." She is someone who fears being regarded as unworthy of love and is desperately afraid of being alone. Plant medicine reveals all of our shadows, all of our hidden pain. I was dissolving my marriage to a man who saw me primarily in a negative light. This was triggering the aspect of my psyche that feared she would never be seen as good or worthy.

I had to acknowledge my bruised heart, and the hunger and longing I had for the experience of deep love. I was engaging a very intense love with Leif now. I felt the lesson was to take responsibility for nourishing that aspect of myself, for no one can satisfy that level of longing. I feel this wounded part in me now and feel her need for love and reassurance. She is an inner-child aspect of my soul. I have begun to engage her in conversation and it has been an eye opener to discover that suppressed pain.

This is an example of how deep this medicine can take you. It brings to one's awareness depths of our being that are ignored in everyday life, yet they linger beneath the surface, yearning for expression. I believe when we acknowledge these parts of ourselves, we can begin to heal. This has far-reaching effects on every aspect of our life.

I was going in and out of consciousness once again and at one point I came to and began experiencing the full-body orgasms of kundalini energy. I was feeling Leif all around me but I didn't have a sense of his actual body. It was as if we were two energy beings experiencing the purest love for each other. The feeling was one of exquisite joy and pleasure in being together. I was telling him how much I loved him, how beautiful he was, how sweet. We were deep in a place of mutual adoration and love.

Again I slipped away into unconsciousness and when I awoke I felt myself as the Earth, changing seasons. I felt myself as winter at that point, cold and soporific. Leif was asking me to come out into the moonlight and sit in the hot tub with him. I had the sense that I was the moon and he was Spirit, calling me out of my dark slumber. Finally, I agreed and he picked me up and carried me into the frigid, clear, moonlit night.

In that moment, everything changed abruptly. Something came over me and I fought to get out of his arms. He let me go and when I looked up at him I saw the most beautiful and terrible sight. Illuminated by the moon, Leif was the figure of Pan standing before me. Bare-chested and very muscular, he had the beard and the horns and these extraordinary, hairy goat legs. Only this was not a friendly Pan. He asked me, "Who do you think I am?" And when he spoke I saw fanged teeth. I was terrified.

When I get scared, I do not scream or run. I usually stand and fight, but in that moment I rushed to the door to get inside, away from him and the freezing cold air. Once inside, I fell to the floor in a ball, shivering from the cold. I could not find a blanket and I was deep in the rabbit hole of the medicine. The entire room looked dank and dark to me. I wondered if I was Persephone, trapped in Hades with a demon guardian. In my mind, Leif had become this beast and I prayed he would turn back into the Leif I knew. Instead, he became more demonic and beast-like.

Leif came back inside wet and cold from the hot tub. I asked him to hold me, thinking that he would somehow remember himself and be restored to normal. He was soaking wet and I felt no solace. I was horrified when I felt coarse, furry legs against mine. I felt his feet as cloven hooves, which sent a chill through my body.

He got up and said, "You have something dark in you." He proceeded to use bamboo leaves to wave away the energy, but he told me later he felt deep hatred from me and stopped. I, on the other hand, saw him as this demonic beast that seemed to be mocking my shamanism as he waved the bamboo leaves around. It was a very scary sight to see this shadowy figure in the dark, waving a grassy frond at me.

Again, I asked him to lie down and hold me. This time I began to feel the life being sucked out of me. I experienced a level of thirst I have never ever felt before. I thought I was in a death throe. The shocking thing was that I was completely resigned. I am such a warrior in real life and here I was at a complete loss. I didn't even open my mouth to ask for water.

Leif had no idea what I was experiencing. He was having his own experience and was utterly confused by how I was behaving. He kept asking me to come out in the moonlight and sit with him in the hot tub. I kept saying no, which made him think I was somehow testing his love by keeping him away from the beautiful moon.

And there is the argument for doing this medicine alone. You do not know where the other person is and this can get very confusing. However, I know there are no mistakes here. We were definitely meant to have this experience together. We would come to learn a tremendous amount from it.

As I was lying on the floor, with Leif holding me, I could see his hand in front of me. It was elongated and bent and hellish looking. I began to feel myself morphing into a beast-like creature as well. My waist felt like it was thickening. My hair felt dry and dead. My hands were elongated and bent. I finally got up to go to the kitchen, but again, all the lights were off and the place looked like a dank, dark prison. I looked out the kitchen window and saw white frost everywhere and was further convinced that I was in some cold underworld. I felt loathing for this demon thing I saw in Leif.

In my mind, I was convinced that this had all been a horrible deception. Leif was gone and replaced by this demon beast that had sucked me so dry I was now a ruin. I thought I would never see my friends and family again. I asked where the phone was and Leif, looking at the late hour, told me that it might not be such a good idea to call anyone right now. I took this to mean that I was stuck there forever.

Leif told me later that I had approached his dog, Charlie, who adored me. This sweet, friendly creature actually growled and almost snapped at me, according to Leif. Animals can sense spirits, and this dog knew there was something very wrong with me.

I demanded to know where the ring was that I'd given Leif. I was very confused. I really thought I had been deceived. I cannot emphasize how much I believed that this was my lot *and I was never going to return to myself. I felt a burning distrust and anger for this being I saw in Leif.*

The next thing I remember, we were sitting on the sofa in the dark and I was tuning into this demonic being. I could feel his darkness, his cold, callous persona. I was despondent that he was unmoved by the love and beauty that I knew I carried. I felt hopeless, knowing there would be no way to get any kind of mercy from it. I asked despondently, "Where is the beauty?"

The next thing I remember, Leif had turned on the light in the living room. He reached up to dim it and by now I was back to myself but badly shaken. I said harshly, "Don't dim that light!! I want to see you!"

He looked at me, utterly at a loss. Then I said, "Never again, Leif! That was *horrible!*" Leif hung his head and began to cry. In that moment I realized he had known nothing about what I was experiencing. I realized that he had been in his own hellish version of it, feeling the sting of mistrust, anger, and hatred being directed at him out of nowhere, and I felt horrible.

I knelt down and held him and told him that something terrible had come into me and marred my perception of him. I began explaining what I'd been experiencing. We decided to go out to the hot tub and sit in the moonlight. As we went outside, Leif put his hand on the doorknob to make sure we wouldn't be locked out and I reached out to make sure he wasn't locking it. I was still a little unsure of him. That is how penetrating the experience had been.

In the hot tub, under a radiant moon that lit up the frost around us, we began to share our experience. We were both emotionally drained from it. Leif had had a powerful journey earlier on the mushrooms and was in a totally different place. When I turned on him he was taken completely off guard. We began to piece it all together and then I lay on my back in the water, surrendering myself to Grandmother Moon. I asked her what on Earth had happened to us.

Before I could finish the question the words came in: "*Succubus, a high adept, black magician. An opportunist, drawn to your light.*" I got that it came in just after our love session we had experienced on the medicine. The energy Leif and I had created with that piece could be felt light-years away by this thing. It was a demon and it had come to feed and mess with us. This was like sport. It was a grand game and I had been totally deceived. I had also been sucked almost dry and I was feeling very drained.

When we finally went to bed, I lay awake for another hour or so thinking about the experience. First I called in Archangel Raphael, the healer, and asked him to clear the tube that connects me to my over-soul so that I may draw in light and regain my energy.

I then called in Archangel Michael, who wields the sword that cuts through all negativity. I asked him to cut away any remnants of that dark energy and keep us protected.

Then I began to look at this demon as a shadow aspect of myself. I knew the only way I could do such a thing would be through the heart center. I brought myself to that place within me and began to ponder the succubus.

What is a succubus? It is a type of demonic vampire that comes in and sucks our light. I considered myself to be a light being and this demon would be the polar opposite of what I was about. I would never have thought of something this demonic as being a shadow aspect of myself. But from a greater perspective, from the perspective of the heart center, which is our spark of the Divine, we are the *all* of it. We are the dark and the light and they are both sacred.

There is a form of shamanic work I do that is called compassionate de-possession. Betsy Bergstrom, a highly respected shaman in the Seattle area, put this soul work forward. I was taught the modality by one of her students, Gabriella Sugier. The work is based on the knowledge that all spirits have the spark of the Divine within them. It is about helping them to return to Source. I thought about how this entity felt to me—cold, calculating, hateful. If it was attached to a client I was working with, it would no doubt be a most challenging and unpleasant de-possession experience. Yet my approach with it would be firm *and* compassionate.

In this case, I was personally victimized by it. I had to let go of my childish desire to track it down and kick its demon ass. I had to ask myself how it served. Firstly, what had it done to us? It had disrupted a beautiful event. It had violated us by playing with our emotions and altering the absolute trust we shared with each other. It frightened and deceived me.

How did it serve? Lying there in bed, I knew it had come in as a teaching for me. Neither of us had been physically harmed in the process. I had the grandmothers around me as well as my great cat, and yet it still made its way in. The event felt almost sanctioned in a way, so I knew this was providing a teaching.

I see many people in a place of preference with regard to anything they perceive as dark or negative. They are all about love and light and they abhor any negativity, to the point where they will deny their own feelings if they are not deemed loving. That denial of the more base emotions only gives more energy to them as they continue to build up, unexpressed. This is true for the whole dark/light continuum. That which we resist, persists.

If I can come into a greater understanding of the demon, then it loses its charge and therefore its ability to exert power over me. In addition, I can view it as a shadow part of myself. This gives me a more expanded understanding of how it ticks. This is key if I'm going to be encountering these energies in de-possession work. In addition, if I am going to be allowing spirits to enter me during my medicine journeys, I had best be able to recognize a demonic frequency. I did not want to experience that again.

I lay in bed thinking about the succubus and how many of us draw or suck from each other both consciously and unconsciously. I have done so. And many of us have played with another's emotions in an uncaring manner at one time or another. Guilty. How many of us have desired to hurt, to harm, to frighten, and to deceive? I was seeing that there was much I had in common with this demon. These were certainly not behaviors that I engaged now, but I had definitely expressed them in some manner over the course of my life.

Granted, there are some beings that are so far gone in the opposite direction that they are in a state of profound forgetting. These entities easily fit the criteria for evil. And yet, viewing them from the heart center takes us out of judgment and fear and opens us to an expanded place of understanding. It doesn't mean we try to engage that kind of energy, but it helps us to begin to understand it.

Another part of the teaching was the newfound awareness that traversing these realms was akin to exploring a big city. You had to be somewhat streetwise. There will always be others who are cleverer and far more experienced. And there are often eyes upon us that we are blithely unaware of that include pranksters and villains. It is naïve to think that the spirit world is exclusively love and light. Tuning into the terrain is good training for any initiate on this path. Setting boundaries and working with guardians is essential.

And with that thought, my eyes wide open in the darkness, I saw an image of my mesa hovering before me. For my first year of shamanic training, I had put four sets of three stones in this medicine bundle. The stones were instruments for healing. I watched as three luminous white stones floated above my mesa and gently drifted downward into the bundle. It was confirmation from Spirit that I was learning the lessons well. I immediately fell into a deep, sound sleep.

⤳ 13 ⤳

Heartbreak

The saddest thing in the world is loving someone who used to love you.

—Anonymous

A fter the succubus debacle, which shook both of us, I had planned to visit Leif the week after Christmas. My girls would be with their dad, so I was free to be with my beloved for the entire week. We had no interest in doing more medicine. The plan was to spend time together relaxing and exploring in the mossy forests that surrounded his home.

I packed bags of groceries from my local organic co-op along with recipes for delicious meals I planned to make. One of my favorite things to do with Leif was cook with him in his kitchen. There was a sweet joy in spending time together preparing a gorgeous meal. We would sit side-by-side on a burl-wood bench and dig into our creation. I would always receive an enthusiastic kiss from him when we were finished.

I had arrived with a beautiful gift for Leif. I had commissioned my friend, Joseph, to make a medicine-gathering bag of elk and bison hide with a wolf foot and frog bells attached to the front. It was for collecting wild mushrooms and I thought Leif would love it.

I arrived the day after Christmas, only to feel him as distant and cool. He expressed no interest in my bags of offerings. He was more concerned with cleaning up the place, as he'd been building bookshelves in the living room before I arrived. There was an awkward silence between us and he made no attempt to take me into his arms as he had every other time I'd arrived.

I could finally stand it no more and asked him what was wrong. He answered coldly that he needed space, that he was in a dark place and that it was winter and he just wanted to hole up alone. He wanted to take the month of January off from seeing me and said he wished to conserve his jing—his male energy. He chastised me for not figuring it out since I was reading Mantak Chia, who is an expert on Taoist sexual practices. This was preposterous, and I sat there stunned, trying not to come apart.

He also told me that he did not miss me when I was gone, explaining that he wanted to be fully present to life and if he was missing someone he was not in the moment. He was rather callous in his exchange with me, at one point asking, "What do you want from me?" I was shocked at such a question. I had not seen this coming. I was totally blindsided.

There had been no mention of any of this in the conversations leading up to my visit. Had I known how he was feeling, I would have never come. What was particularly upsetting, aside from his cold distance, was that it came from left field. Two weeks ago he was excited to have me in his home. He was affectionate and engaging and happy. I didn't recognize him now.

I spent the night in his bed quietly weeping as he slept next to me. He had barely touched me and my heart was breaking. I knew this was because of our last medicine experience. We had both been traumatized by that journey and Leif was really thrown by my behavior toward him. It clearly affected him deeply, for he was a changed person with me now.

Leif was guarded and almost resentful of me. It felt like he didn't trust me, and at certain moments throughout that week, I wondered if he even liked me.

When we awoke the next morning I cried as we talked more about it. He was still very cool and rather flippant with me. I kept explaining that I was unprepared for this sudden change of heart and I was struggling with feelings of hurt, but he was not hearing it. I could not reach him and I could feel my desperation creeping in.

Nothing was resolved, and I spent the better part of the day in a stupor of emotional pain while Leif remained distant. At some point he handed me a bunch of envelopes, each with a gift certificate for Maya abdominal massage, which I loved. I looked for a card but none had been given. A simple, "Love, L" was written on one of the envelopes. I was grateful for the generous gift and at the same time a bit hurt that he'd not included a card. This was someone who had just a few weeks earlier written six haikus for me.

Later in the day we sat down to open his presents. I had found a particularly beautiful card with a dragon silk-screened on the cover. I'd written him a haiku and a very sentimental letter. I sat with tears streaming down my cheeks as he read it, feeling like my words were all for naught. When he opened my gift, however, he appeared genuinely touched.

He came over to me and asked why I was still crying.

"I just want to get all of this straight," I responded. "When I leave here I will not be asked back any time soon. I will not be missed. And you are saving your jing because it's winter and I was supposed to have figured that out on my own because I'm reading Mantak Chia."

He laughed, saying he loved me and joked that he wasn't planning on holding back *all* his jing. He took me to the bedroom to prove his point.

Unfortunately, his distance never really resolved itself. We went to the ocean with heavy wet suits and played in the freezing waves. We hiked beautiful trails, and as the week wore on I could feel him continuing to pull away. I had the feeling he was trying to keep me entertained and was looking forward to his solitude.

The day before I was to leave, we went for a long walk. I turned to him and told him that I would honor his need to be alone for January. I told him I was struggling because of how close we had felt until just this week. I reminded him that he had told me he was attached to me.

He turned to me and practically hissed, "I don't want to be attached to anyone!" That did it. I turned and walked briskly back to the car. I knew I had overstayed my welcome and that I was to leave when we got back to the house.

My departure was met with callous comments that stung me with their cruel sarcasm. He was insisting I stay and not drive in the dark, but at the same time he was pushing me away with mean words.

The final remark shattered my heart. I hugged him and said, "I just want my Leif back. The one who's crazy about me, and can't wait to see me."

"He was on mushrooms," he responded.

It was all I could do to get out of the house.

I felt an overwhelming emptiness that was almost unbearable. I was returning to a home I was sharing with a husband I was divorcing. There was no money at that time for me to move out or buy a car. I had a busy teaching schedule coming up and was hopeful that I could make it my livelihood, but nothing was for sure. Leif had brought me a joy I had not felt in years and had touched my heart deeply. I felt profoundly lonely and sad.

At the same time I knew he loved me. I had more consciousness than to go into victimhood and anger, thinking he was the bad guy. He needed space, it was clear. I would respect that need. I would not call or email him. It was probably the best thing for both of us.

When someone requests space I must honor it, even though it triggers my own abandonment issues. I knew that compassion, not reaction was the way to go here. Leif had his defenses up the entire week. Underneath defense is fear. In knowing this, I could feel compassion for him rather than going into my own reaction.

My sadness was excruciating but I had tools to help me bear it. I wanted to stay conscious through this very painful experience and not spiral into my own self-centered fears. I could not bear to lose Leif, but I had to let him go.

When I got home that night I pulled out my bag of Nordic Runes. I put my hand inside and asked the question, "Will Leif come back to me in love?" The rune I pulled was called Jera, meaning harvest—a fertile season. It was a rune of "beneficial outcomes" according to Ralph Blum's *Book of Runes*. The book explained that a period of time must pass before reaping the harvest. It went on to say, "You have prepared the ground and planted the seed. Now you must cultivate with care."

I had been a friend of Leif's for almost three years. We had experienced deep love for the past five months. I could only hope the foundation was there to support a return to each other.

❧ 14 ❧

Engaging the Pain

What keeps us alive, what allows us to endure?
I think it is the hope of loving, or being loved.
I heard a fable once about the sun going on a journey to
find its source, and how the moon wept without her lover's
warm gaze.
We weep when light does not reach our hearts. We wither
like fields if someone close to us does not rain their kindness
upon us.

—Meister Eckhart, *The Hope of Loving*

Suffering will transform us if we have the fortitude to look within and endeavor to truly learn from it. It is my least favorite mode of learning but it does shift me quite effectively. There is a wonderful quote in Michael Roads' book, *Talking With Nature*, that says, "Without pain, joy becomes shallow. Without the falling to earth there can be no transcendent light."

I had officially entered a dark night of the soul around relationship. That first week back I was overwhelmed with emotional pain. It was all I could do to function during the day. The pain was so great it was difficult to take a deep breath. I could barely eat, but I made sure that what little I put in my body was nutrient-dense, as I needed my energy to take care of my girls and get through the day.

Nights were the most difficult, as I was alone in my bed with nothing to distract me. My first night back I barely slept and Monday was a blur of despair. Monday night, I was in a bad way. I knew I had to do something or I would be up through the night. I thought about my mushroom journeys where I would sink into Mother Earth and become infused with her energy. I decided to try it in my bedroom. I had nothing to lose.

I imagined myself lying on a bed of soft green moss. I began to sink downward into the moss and I called up Mother Earth to enfold me with her love. I was completely focused on this. I gave myself over to her and I began to feel her energy filling me, surrounding me, comforting me.

Then, I called in the fairies and felt their presence around me, dancing in my field. The experience was as real as it had been on the medicine. I was filled with the presence of love. I was, however, not writhing with kundalini. This was not the time for that. I was lying very still and fully present to the Earth and her medicine. I lay in quiet focus for a long time. The next thing I knew, it was morning.

I awoke sad but surprised and grateful to have received a full night's rest. I had barely slept at Leif's house the past week and my body was desperate for the nourishment of sleep. Sinking into the moss and calling Mother Earth became my nightly practice for the rest of the month. It was the only way I could get to sleep.

It was surprising that I had stayed the entire week with Leif. It had been beyond painful for me. In my mind I thought he would turn around, yet he only became more distant and resentful of my presence. I knew I had to honor his request for space now. That day I received a brief email from him. He apologized and said he never meant to hurt my feelings. He thanked me for the gifts and said he loved me very much.

I responded simply by saying that it was a difficult week. I thanked him for the massages and said that I loved him and would respect his need for space. I left it at that.

That first week, I checked my phone and email during the day and evening for any further contact from him, but none came. It crushed me. There was no choice but to let him go and try to learn from it.

I've always been resourceful, and I knew it was time to place my focus on creating the life I wanted for myself. I was anxious to get out of the house I shared with Richard and get on with my life. I needed to get myself centered and build my teaching so I could support my girls.

I knew a physical outlet would help, so I embraced an intense daily workout that would build strength and endurance. I created a channel to release the heavy emotions from my body. This would also serve to help me feel better about myself.

Getting my finances together was essential so I could buy a car and find a place to rent. I was planning on staying in the house with Richard for another six months till school was over and I was in a better position to leave. I had several classes planned for the next month and I began putting more together. This would help bring in income and nourish my love of teaching women.

As the week wore on, the pain gnawed at me, threatening to devour me entirely. I was fortunate to have a community of wise and compassionate women in my life and I found myself directed to exactly the right friend at the right time.

By Friday I was desperate to connect with Leif. I sat down and typed out a heartfelt letter to him. I planned to wait one more week and then send it to him. In the letter, I wrote that I felt he was seeing me through cold and distant eyes. I went on to essentially plead my case, explaining that my love was true, that I was a friend first, and that this was not some mushroom delusion. I also did the unthinkable and told him what I perceived was happening with him in his decision to retreat, which is rarely well received by anyone.

It was a heartfelt and desperate letter. I made the wise choice to send it to my friend Nina, to see what she thought. She called me the following day, saying that under no circumstances should I send him that letter unless I wanted to destroy any chance of getting back together. I had promised Leif his space for January. I could not contact him. He clearly needed it and I had to respect that.

I realized that I had reverted to a young, needy, grasping part of myself that was desperate to hang on, certain that she could convince him to want me. I had to address this part of myself and not just intellectually. I would have to work with her consistently. She had been with me most of my life and it was time to heal her.

Nina told me that this was my opportunity to go deeply into my pain and engage it, give it voice, and see what it needed. It was a chance for me to shift an old pattern that had run its course. I knew that if I didn't take the time to do this, I would revert back to these old behaviors and the possibility of a deep love relationship would elude me forever.

She also said that what I needed to learn here was self-control. I sometimes overwhelmed people in my exuberance. There was a part of me that was so damn glad to have someone love me that I gave too much. It was as if I was trying to validate myself to them that I am lovable, all the while praying they would not discover the parts of me I felt shame over. It was those parts that required my attention and love.

Those unhealed aspects were coming forward in my mushroom journeys, particularly the journey in December. I had cried to Leif that I "danced the dance of the good daughter" for him. I was projecting a male authority onto him and pleading with him to accept me. I had to address those aspects.

Saturday night, both my girls were at sleepovers. I walked down the hall to my bedroom, journal in hand, and closed the door. I dropped down to the floor and wailed to Mother Earth. I gave my pain voice and released a torrent of agonized sobs.

When I calmed down, I wrote in my journal, "My pain, I am listening. Talk to me. Tell me what you need."

It answered, "I want to be loved fiercely. I want someone to see me as precious. I want to be thought of as worth fighting for. I want a deep connection with a man."

I then wrote, "That is beautiful. You deserve that and more."

My pain responded with, "I am so sad and lonely now. I miss his love. I miss his protective caring. I miss his desire for me. I feel I was not enough for him. I feel I am not enough for anyone."

I told my pain that if we gave him some time, he might come back with greater appreciation than before. And if he didn't, then it was never meant to be. I said I would tend to its needs. I would give my pain voice and I would create a life where I was sustained by my connection to nature, which was a source of unlimited beauty and inspiration for me.

Through the mushroom journeys I was forging a bond with the nature spirits. I had a deep reverence for the natural world, often saying that it was the only technology I really understood. I would reach into Mother Earth to nourish and love me, particularly the parts of myself that were starved for love.

I climbed into bed and spent the next two hours reading *Talking With Nature*. I soaked up his wisdom hungrily. At one point, as I neared the bottom of a page, an owl outside my window began hooting. I turned the page and to my astonishment, there was a drawing of an owl.

With the mystical nature spirits of Michael Roads' book stirring my imagination, I fell asleep. I was awakened the following morning by the owl hooting yet again. It was seven-thirty a.m. and I had slept nine hours in peaceful slumber.

A realization hit me that morning. Leif was a catalytic force in my life. He was the necessary catalyst that inspired me to end my broken marriage. Now he was the necessary catalyst to make me address and heal my deepest wounds. Spirit had put someone in my life so rare and unique that my heart would fully open. This would not have happened with just anyone.

There was a window of opportunity to face these wounds and initiate powerful work on behalf of myself. I was in that place of pain where full surrender is not only possible—it is the only choice. I wanted joy and love in my life. It was not Leif's job to give me that happiness. It was available to me at any time. It was always a choice. How often had I chosen to hurt instead?

Being a capable person with many gifts to utilize, I could choose to create abundance and joy in my life. I began my inner work by addressing Mother Earth as her daughter. I asked her to fill me with her love and to heal my heart. I asked her to send me her children who would benefit most from my teaching. And I asked her to look out for me, promising to stay open to her guidance.

Keeping a journal on a daily basis allowed me to check in with my pain. I gave it voice through sound and movement that I had learned from a teacher years back. This was particularly powerful and I was often surprised by what came out of me. Releasing that energy was imperative as every emotion that is suppressed ends up somewhere in the body. I wanted to be able to move forward, unhindered by the past.

It amazes me what we are capable of repressing within ourselves. We do it so often we don't even realize the gravity of what we are carrying. It creates radical imbalance within us and ultimately results in illness and disease. I did not want to carry the burden of unhealed wounds and old behavior patterns any longer. I made a decision that I was finished with self-created suffering. I would endeavor to make this year a year of deep healing, self-love, and growth.

A day later, Leif contacted me, apologizing. He was sincere, and rather than sink into old behavior where I would stay in victim, I accepted his apology. I made a request of him that the next time he needed space he would simply say so and spare me what I had to endure after Christmas.

Our shared medicine journeys had cracked open our psyches and put us in very vulnerable territory with each other. It had become all too much for him and he responded the way he responded. I told him I wished always to be a soft place for him to land, and that I held his heart with care and reverence. I acknowledged his wisdom in taking time apart for the month of January.

Throughout the month, I was dogged by emotional pain. I had definitely not recovered from that horrible week together. I had never in my life been this heartbroken. I knew that in reality this was a gift, taking me back to my core wounds. I pondered the patterns that were playing out in my life around my love relationships. My soon-to-be-ex-husband had not fought to keep me, which had hurt. He had not fought for me over the past few years either, favoring his kids at all costs. I had shed many tears over that. Now Leif had retracted his affections suddenly, after a period of intense love and bonding. I was struck by how much this pattern seemed to resemble my first few months of life. My birth mother had kept me for the first five months and then gave me up for adoption. In the first six months of life, a baby has no concept of being separate. This had to have had an effect on my deep psyche. How interesting to see that pattern playing itself out at this time in my life.

At the same time I was dealing with losing Leif's affections, Richard and I officially filed for divorce, setting into motion the end of this chapter in our lives. Sitting in the lawyer's office felt surreal. Here I was, ending my marriage, but it felt more like I was checking off my to-do list. I was long over the pain of my marriage failing. I rode home in the car silently grieving the loss of what I'd had with Leif. I was marveling darkly at all the things that were falling away in my life. I felt like I had no skin left on me.

Later that week, I had a session with Diana, my therapist, who was a gifted healer. We talked about pain and how it serves. I was in too much of it as far as I was concerned and I was doing everything I could to navigate through it.

At the same time I was lamenting the cruelty of the gods for giving me a taste of such bonding, such love, and then removing it in the harshest way. I was bereft at this point.

Diana explained that the purpose of pain is to hollow out the container so one can hold more grace and love. It creates a different kind of capacity within. She said the pain burns in the chest and in doing so it creates an opening within that would not have been opened otherwise. This level of pain serves to deepen you. You are now working from a heightened place.

Most mystics have experienced significant pain. Diana told me the story of the great Sufi poet, Rumi. Rumi did not write a poem until after he experienced crippling pain. He was a scholar, married with children, and he was revered in his town.

A wandering dervish named Shams showed up one day. Shams felt he'd been guided there to find a spiritual partner with whom to delve more deeply into the mystery. He met Rumi and they fell in love in a way that was all-encompassing and totally transforming. Whether or not this was physical is speculative at best. They were inseparable and their connection was profound.

Rumi had a collection of books that he prized highly. There is a story that Shams threw all of his books into a fountain, telling Rumi he can follow that path or he can simply *"know, experience."* Rumi answered, saying that he would choose the path of knowing. Shams pulled all the books out of the fountain and they were dry.

Eventually, the townspeople who revered Rumi became jealous of the relationship. Rumi's son and some other men conspired together and killed Shams. Rumi was devastated. He engaged his pain by writing some of the most exquisite poetry ever put forth. His poems are about

ιe love of the beloved. Shortly after his loss, Rumi began
) experience God in everything.

Diana finished the story by saying, "That level of
expression only comes about through the experiencing
of profound pain." She then read a poem by Rumi that
touched my heart and summoned tears to my cheeks.

The Way Wings Should

*What will our children do in the morning? Will they wake
with their hearts wanting to play the way wings should?
Will they have dreamed the needed flights and gathered the
strength from the planets that all men and women need
to balance the wonderful charms of the earth so that her
power and beauty does not make us forget our own?
I know all about the ways of the heart—how it wants to
be alive.
Love so needs to love that it will endure almost anything,
even abuse, just to flicker for a moment.
But the sky's mouth is kind, its song will never hurt you,
for I sing those words.
What will our children do in the morning, if they do not
see us fly?*

—Rumi

☞ 15 ☜

Daughter Who Knows

The Greeks used the term pharmacotheon or "divine drug."
This sort of psychotropic compound differs from the opi-
ates, such as morphine and heroin, and from such stimu-
lants as cocaine, in that it does not produce addiction and
acts specifically on human consciousness. As a matter of
fact, under specific internal and external conditions, this
class of drugs, whether called hallucinogens, psychedelics,
or entheogens, is capable of producing a totality experience,
the unio-mystica.
— Carl A. P. Ruck, R. Gordon Wasson,
Albert Hofmann, *The Road to Eleusis: Unveiling the*
Secret of the Mysteries

What I am about to share is deeply sacred. I write this in the spirit of showing what is possible on this powerful medicine path. A series of synchronistic events led up to this particular journey, culminating in the most extraordinary and transformative experience I have ever had in my life.

I had planned to do a solo journey on January 20th. It would be my first time doing the medicine alone. My girls would be with their dad that weekend. Richard would be home, but he'd be busy readying the other end of the house for a group he was hosting the next day.

Ten days before my journey, I had a powerful dream. Dreams have different qualities to them and this one got my attention. Here is the dream:

I am in a church-like setting. There is a priest up at the front. It is time for communion. My row moves to the center aisle and we make our way toward the priest. Before I reach him he leaves and my friend Zora replaces him as priestess.

I stand before her and I am holding a cracked-open egg-shell filled with the egg as well as three baby spiders. Zora blesses it and then I drink the whole thing. I am wearing white with a red sash around my waist. I walk away realizing that I just swallowed three spiders and I wasn't repelled. I'm aware in the dream that this is a sacred act.

In the dream the sacred masculine has led up to this point, and is then replaced by the sacred feminine, the priestess. The dream is announcing that the sacred feminine within me is taking over now. I looked up the meaning of the name, Zora, and it means "dawn," which heralds a new beginning, a rebirth. The egg is an alchemical container that holds highly transformative forces within. It is a symbol of birth and new beginnings. The spider is a powerful symbol of the feminine and it is the weaver. I saw the three baby spiders as symbols of the new web I am weaving as I create my new life for my two daughters and myself.

I also saw the three spiders as symbols of the three faces of the feminine—maiden, mother, and crone. I felt the dream was also announcing my birth into this third phase of my life, as the crone/wise woman.

My drinking the egg and the spiders was my accepting of this new beginning. In the Catholic Church, communion is a sacrament and that is what I was engaging.

The red sash around my waist represented the moon blood I am now holding inside me. The white is another symbol of new life and purity.

I feel this dream is linked to the medicine journey I was to experience. The day after I had the dream, I had a session with my therapist/healer, Diana. We worked with the dream and then I told her I would be doing a solo medicine journey the following week. Diana advised me to let a friend know what I would be doing so I would have someone out there who knew to check in on me.

I asked my friend and neighbor, Sasha, if I could call her if needed and she happily agreed. She was a dear friend and I trusted her implicitly. The week before I was to do the medicine, I phoned my midwife friend, Amelia, who had taken the medicine with me the previous month. I told her I would be doing the medicine that Friday and she immediately told me to call her if I needed her. She said she would set aside that evening to be there for me. I made sure I had her number, but I didn't think I would be calling her as I had Sasha lined up already.

The Monday after that weekend I would be hosting a White Owl Medicine Healing on the new moon for a group of women in my community. Joseph had been working on my white owl fan and would be sending it to me any day. I was hoping to work with it a bit before the ceremony to align myself with its medicine.

In divine timing, the fan arrived on Friday, the day of my medicine journey. I took it out of the box and it was more beautiful than I had imagined. Joseph was a master beader and the beading on the handle was exquisite. The feathers had an ethereal quality to them. I was very taken by the fan. It had a totally different quality to it compared to the other medicine pieces I'd worked with.

Outside my home a blanket of thick white snow covered every inch of my beautiful land. It had the look of an enchanted Avalon forest, giving me a feeling of being insulated and held.

Around three-thirty, I went into my soft green room, bringing my statue of Ix Chel, the Earth Mother, my sage, and my white owl fan. I lit the sage and cleared the room with the fan, asking for white owl to come in and protect and guide me. I smudged myself with the sage and then sat down to eat five grams of the mushrooms. I was nervous about going it completely alone but I knew I was to go all the way with this.

A half-hour or so later I felt the medicine begin to kick in. I said to the mushrooms, "Please hear me. I come to you with no skin left, just my wounded heart. I ask you, please. Be gentle with me. I come to you for your counsel and your teaching."

When the effects of the medicine come on, it talks to me in a rhyming singsong way. It responded, saying, "Let go. Let go. We are friend, not foe!" I felt an immediate sense of smiling friendliness and I knew I would be taken care of.

Almost immediately, I saw a white sphere in the distance making its way to me. As it neared I saw it had wings and then I realized it was the white owl. She stood before me and became a beautiful woman clothed in white owl feathers with long, flowing white hair. She radiated warmth and kindness, and said, "I am White Owl. I am your medicine and I will work with you, Daughter Who Longs."

My heart opened to her and I radiated my gratitude. I opened my eyes in that moment and my entire bedroom was encased in luminous white owl feathers. It was such a beautiful sight to behold. I was completely contained and protected. She was to be my guardian throughout the entire journey and her love for me was beyond anything I could possibly describe in words.

As the journey progressed, tears came to me intermittently and I let myself cry. At different times I heard noises outside my bedroom. Richard was making dinner in the kitchen and at times he was in and out of the living room. As that happened, I felt a large wing fold me into White Owl's breast in the same way a mother owl would hold a fledgling to her when danger is near. My crying would cease and I would sit in the quiet of soft feathers until he moved out of hearing distance.

I heard snow melting and falling from the roof outside my window. As each clump of snow fell away, I felt myself releasing old energy along with it. At one point a large piece crashed from the roof and White Owl joked, "That was a particularly big piece for you, Daughter Who Longs."

Mother Earth then drew me into her and I was again called Daughter Who Longs. "Come to me, Daughter Who Longs," she said. "Come into my green glow. Is it any wonder that the color of the heart is green and so also am I? I love you, Daughter Who Longs."

At that she drew me in from the top of a tree, down a spider web of branches that held fall leaves of yellow, down the trunk and into the luminous green Earth.

I remember having my hands on my rather bony hips at this point and Mother Earth said to me, "You must eat, Daughter Who Longs. You are starving yourself. You must eat, Daughter Who Is Dying."

This startled me and I looked at her and she said, "Yes, daughter. You must know. The girl in you must die." I began to cry. I understood then why the tree had yellow leaves. It was a time of shedding, of passing from one phase into another.

I cried and cried, and then said, "I don't want to lose my vitality. I don't want to lose my beauty. I don't want to die."

Instantly White Owl Goddess was standing in front of me. She was smiling. She put her beautiful hands over my heart chakra and looked into my eyes with her warmth and her love, saying, "Daughter Who Longs, you will have a deeper beauty—a deeper beauty. It will come from in here." I felt the energy from her hands filling my heart.

"You will be birthed tonight," she continued. "You will be birthed from Daughter Who Longs to Daughter Who Knows. I will help you." At that she took me to a place where we were standing in a landscape of crystalline white snow.

She stood before me and said, "I am removing the veils, goddess." She removed two veils from me. I was incredulous that she called me "goddess" and she laughed and said, "Yes! You are a goddess! You are my sister. I will work with you not as something greater than yourself. I will work with you as your sister."

I felt myself radiating luminous blue light when the veils came off. Then I was catapulted into what I can only describe as the Cosmos, the Universe, the All.

The voice of the Mother said to me, "You are a part of this, Daughter Who Longs." I was shown sweeping landscapes of earthly beauty and she said, "You are a part of this. You are That and It is You." I was shown beauty of such magnitude and scope I could never hope to express in words. It is beyond my capacity of expression.

At some point I was welcomed very deeply into the heart of the Mother. I had a moment where I feared losing myself but the Mother said, "Do not be afraid, Daughter Who Longs. You are welcome here. Let yourself go. Come dance in my love." It was an experience of beauty that is again beyond my ability to convey.

After this I found myself beginning to experience an intensity I recognized from previous journeys. I was deep, deep in the medicine and I was without a body, completely dissolved. It was similar to the experience I had with Leif where I was between worlds. It is a very strange place. It feels like a realm I return to and the "reality" of my life is gone. It's like I'm in some kind of holding pattern and I have no guarantee I will return to this life. It is a feeling of my identity slipping away from me completely and I have no sense of what is "real."

I fought this and ventured out of my room into the hallway where I made my way to my daughter's room to grab my cellphone. I needed to call Sasha and make sure this was not all a dream. I wanted to know that "I" was really "real" and not some diaphanous dream. I wanted to make sure Sasha really existed. I called her and her phone rang and rang and rang. The answering machine never picked up, it just kept ringing with no answer. I was afraid this meant that my "reality" was lost to me.

I felt the presence of White Owl and I knew she was directing this. Then I remembered Amelia and I called her. To my great relief she answered. I said, "Hey, Amelia. I'm in a place of need. I need to hear your voice." Her voice was reassuring and calm and she said, "Yeah, I know that place. I'm here for you, Shonagh. How are you doing?"

I told her about White Owl. I said she wouldn't believe how beautiful my room is, encased in luminous white owl feathers. I said I was being addressed as "Daughter Who Longs." I began talking about my feeling that I was not enough for someone.

I then spoke about being adopted at that critical stage where there is no concept of separateness. I was really getting that that was my original wounding.

And then the most devastating realization came to me that was beyond anything I could bear alone.

It entered my awareness that I came into this world as someone's burden, and not someone's joy. The realization hit me with the force of a tidal wave and I knew that I had this knowing in utero.

I was racked with sobs that poured from the deepest recesses of my heart. All the while, Amelia stayed calm and said, "Shonagh, you just cry. I'm here to hold this for you." My beautiful friend acted as midwife as I birthed the realization of my original wound and its accompanying pain.

She told me the following day that she felt like she was standing with me on the edge of the abyss of my core wound. She was amazed I went in, saying she knew of no one else who could have done that. She said the courage it took me to go there just blew her mind.

That place within me was a chasm of such awesome, overwhelming pain—I could barely stand it. It was no coincidence that I could not reach Sasha. It seemed that I needed to be midwifed, and Amelia was more than qualified. I have changed her name for this book but she informed me that the meaning of her real name is "Spring." Another reference to rebirth and new beginnings—such a lovely "coincidence."

I am forever indebted to Amelia for what she made possible. When we hung up, I curled up in bed and went back into my journey.

White Owl came to me and said, "It was a good birth. You are now Daughter Who Knows."

I felt myself as a fledgling on the forearm of Pan. He wore the protective leather gauntlet one wears when working with birds of prey. He was talking to Mother Earth and said, "She will fly. I will work with her." Whenever I thought of myself as Daughter Who Longs, he would whisper lovingly, "You are Daughter Who Knows."

He again assured Mother Earth that I would fly, when White Owl appeared before me. She said with authority, "She is Daughter Who Knows and she can fly!"

In that moment I became the white owl and I was soaring in the night sky. I had perfect clarity of vision and my wings were massive and strong. It was a feeling of such freedom and love. My heart was bursting. In that moment I realized I needed no one to be my other wing; I had strong, sturdy wings of my own that could take me to unimaginable heights.

With that realization I found myself being welcomed into a realm of gentle earth spirits. They said, "Come be with us, we welcome you." As I entered their space I brought with me a beautiful golden light.

They continued, "You are an angel. Come rest in our kindness."

I nestled blissfully with these sweet beings and later found myself lucid in my bedroom, still enshrouded in white owl feathers. I looked at White Owl and asked, "Do you think it's okay to call Leif?"

She replied, "You are Daughter Who Knows." Then she smiled and said, "He will listen."

I picked up my phone and struggled to dial his number. The whole time, I held my beautiful white owl fan. When I got through, we began our conversation.

I told him a bit about my journey and then said, "I miss you, Leif. I know you don't 'miss' but I do, and it's not because I am not present in the moment. I just think of you fondly and I miss you. I love you. I know you will think that is the mushrooms talking but really, the mushrooms cut to the truth and my truth is all I have to give. I love who you are and I am ever grateful that you have shared yourself with me, and that you have shared your beautiful home and beautiful land."

"I love you very much, Shonagh, and I miss you."

"I want you to know that I love how you stand so steadfast and loyal to beautiful Mother Earth. You are a guardian of that land of green and I hold that love for the Earth in my heart too. I recognize you, Leif, my heart to yours. I am grateful for your friendship and I will always love you. And magic awaits us in Belize. The green is very rich there and it is calling."

"Yeah, I will need that," Leif replied. "I have no sun here. So I curl up like a worm in the ground and I go into the place you saw me last month. So you've seen that part of me."

"I've seen your shadow, Leif. And I love you still. It is an expression of your beauty. It is a terrible beauty, but it is part of you and I can love it. You cut me deep, Leif. But the press of the knife betrays your own pain and suffering. You are my wounded warrior and my gentle-hearted love. I did the Tonglen breathing for you. Yes, that's it. I took on your suffering, and I breathed into you, my love. That was no small act. I love you beyond words and I can love you without attachment. I see deeply into you, the dark and the light, and it is all beautiful."

"Well, good work on your journey, darlin'. You can call me any time."

I felt awkwardness and at the same time, I knew he had heard me, with his heart. I had spoken from the truth of my heart and I meant every word. I had called him not as Daughter Who Longs, but as Daughter Who Knows. White Owl then told me a healing had occurred between us, and I knew it to be true.

After I hung up, I again curled up and let myself be taken deep into the medicine. My mind then went into worry about my current life situation where money was tight and things were uncertain. Earth Mother said to me, "Gentle Daughter, help is on the way. Do not fret. You will be taken care of."

I then saw myself surrounded by the grandmothers I work with. They radiated gentle love to me. I said to them, "I have been singing you through (channeling) with my crystal bowl. I hope I have done so with the reverence and honoring that you deserve."

"*Daughter, we move through you with love. Call us in at any time.*" Again, tears of gratitude came through me and I let myself be bathed in their healing.

Later I found myself floating in the luminous green light and I wondered to Mother Earth, "Is this folly? How will I possibly be able to write about this experience? How can I ever put this to paper?" She responded saying, "You are Daughter Who Knows. You will remember and you will write."

A little later, as I felt the medicine starting to recede, I called Amelia again. She asked how I was doing and I said, "Well, I'm afraid I called Leif."

She said hesitantly, "Oh no. How did that go?" I repeated what I had said to him and she said, "Shonagh, that is beautiful. You are so beautiful in how you express from your heart. I feel he heard you from his heart, which was a healing for him. You saw his shadow and you can love all of him. That is so powerful."

We talked for a while after that, and I thanked her for the kindness she showed to me that night. She said it was an honor to be there at such a powerful time for me. I joked with her, saying, "Listen, you tell that gorgeous husband of yours that Shonagh said he is to make love to you tonight like his life depends on it!

"You just say, 'Honey, I have midwifed all evening and now it's ME time. You ravage me with all you've got!'" We laughed and talked some more and then I released her to her family.

I looked at the time and it was just nine o'clock. I gave my friend, Sasha, a call and we talked till I was too tired to speak. I lay in bed holding my white owl fan, feeling myself as whole. At one point, I kissed the fan in thanks. Instantly, my phone light lit up, bathing the nightstand in a green glow. It went out just as suddenly and I knew it was her, loving me back.

I slept intermittently at best for the rest of the night. How does one sleep when one has received a grace such as that? I went over the journey in my head, astonished at the gravity and the depth of the experience. I was in a state of awe and humility, and I continue to feel that as I write this page. I feel profoundly changed. I have direct experience now of knowing I am not alone, not ever. I am held and guided with a love beyond description. And as I complete this chapter, an owl hoots outside my window.

☞ 16 ☜

White Owl Medicine

*I know a cure for sadness: Let your hands touch some-
thing that makes your eyes smile. I bet there are a hundred
objects close by that can do that. Look at beauty's gift to
us—her power is so great she enlivens the earth, the sky,
our soul.*

—Kabir, *A Hundred Objects Close By*

My medicine experience shifted me into a state of
deep gratitude. The following night I slept with my
fan next to me on the bedside table. I awoke the next
morning and reached over to touch it. I thought, "Spirit
is with me." No sooner had I considered those words than
an owl began to hoot outside my window. Spirit answered
and I cried in appreciation.

Monday evening I was to host a new-moon ceremony
where I would be offering a White Owl Medicine Healing.
I had asked the women to wear white for the ceremony.
I placed a white blanket in the center of the circle with
three large candles framing it. The candles represented
the three faces of the feminine: maiden, mother, and
crone. I planned to have each woman come to the center of the circle. I would smudge her with sage and use

my white owl fan to send in the medicine. Ten women said they'd attend and to my amazement, twenty-seven women showed up. A couple of women I knew well did a double-take when they saw me, each one saying there was something "different" about me.

When the ceremony began, it was a sight to behold. Twenty-seven mystical women dressed in white surrounded me in circle. I often begin by telling a story when leading ceremony. I told them how the owl had been present for me on my medicine journeys and about my extraordinary experience on the medicine just a few nights before our gathering. I also told them about the shaman who had given me the owl necklace two years earlier.

I then explained that I would be working with one woman at a time in the center of the circle. I had downloaded owl calls from a wonderful CD by the Cornell Laboratory of Ornithology, called *Voices of North American Owls*. This would go for about an hour or so and then I'd play a second CD called *Sacred Chants of Devi: Mother Divine*—all about the Divine Mother.

I turned out the lights and we were bathed in soft candlelight. The owl calls began and I felt myself go into an altered state. The first woman came to the center of the circle. With my full focus and attention on her, I let my hand holding the fan move instinctively as I blew the sage on her. The energy in the room had a very soft and loving feel.

After ten or so women, a very pregnant woman came to the center. She had lost a newborn baby the previous year due to negligence at the birthing hospital. She had tears streaming down her cheeks as I blew sage over her full belly, my fan sending her its healing grace. At some point the owl sounds simply switched off and the CD of sacred chants to the Mother came on. This was no accident. I felt it as a message from Spirit that her baby would be born safe and healthy. (That did indeed happen.) She wrote me later saying that being softly touched by the white owl feathers was like being kissed by the Great Mother.

Each woman I worked on stood before me with an open heart, her eyes closed. There was one woman, an artist, who held my gaze the entire time. I remember looking into her eyes, completely surrendered to the sacredness of the moment. After the ceremony, she came up to me and said, "I want to tell you something. First of all, that was simply beautiful. I looked into your eyes the whole time and I want to tell you, they were not human. They held such a love I could not look away. I have just one question for you. Who are you?" I didn't know how to answer her question. I awkwardly responded that I was still trying to figure that out.

The following morning, White Owl came to me and asked me the same question. I felt the answer come to me from the truth of my heart. "I am Daughter Who Knows. I am White Owl Medicine Woman." It felt almost blasphemous to think such a thing. Who the hell was I? I was certainly not Native American. The truth, however, is that this medicine is available to all who show up with integrity and heart.

My own magical bloodlines are from my Scottish, French, and Celtic ancestry. In that moment I understood that I was ready to step into my power and this was the medicine I was gifted. It was time to carry my gifts with confidence.

That same day, I went to visit my friend, Kara. She was the friend who generously lent me her car every month so I could be with Leif. As I sat in her kitchen and told her about my medicine journey with White Owl, she said to me, "Wait a minute. I have something I've been saving for you." She left the room and returned holding the most beautiful burl-framed Audubon print of a pair of snowy white owls. I burst out crying.

It was a magnificent picture. I loved that it was a pair. It felt to me like a representation of the sacred masculine and the sacred feminine—the mysteries in perfect harmony. I told Kara that it would go on my altar to be treasured forever. I was shaking with emotion at this point, and could not believe how powerfully white owl was calling to me. The caliber of friends surrounding me at this time was just staggering. I felt blessed at every turn.

Kara was a longtime initiate within a sacred order. She was also a gifted intuitive and energetic adept. We talked about how I had approached the medicine that night, in a state of surrender, with "no skin left, just my wounded heart." She told me that this is the most powerful way to approach sacred initiation. No ego, no defenses, no resistance—just the truth of one's heart, whatever that may be. She said that I would not have been accessible to such a numinous experience if I hadn't been so completely open and vulnerable. I understood perfectly.

Leaving with my beautiful white owl print, I marveled at the synchronicity playing out in my life. When I got home I placed it on my altar, leaning it against the wall. I had an arched branch covered in lichen that I'd found earlier, and I placed that just in front of the owls. It was my offering of an extra perch should they want it. My owl fan sat in the clutch of a conch shell, which is used in sacred ceremony—my shaman teacher had found it for me. The priest or priestess blows through the shell, opening the directions. I felt the energy in my office/sacred space as balanced and calm.

As the week progressed, I continued to engage White Owl, calling to her before I fell asleep and working with her during the day. The nights were still difficult for me. The overwhelming feeling of emptiness would find me and I would call in the moss and Mother Earth. I would call to my White Owl sister to work with me while I slept, asking her for clarity and insight.

On Friday I spent the better part of the day editing and filling in earlier chapters of this book. The memories of my time spent with Leif before December spun me into more grief and sorrow.

Although we'd spoken on the phone once that week, there were no effusive emails, nor any messages on my voicemail. I knew he was back in town. His mother lived in my area and Leif would come back regularly to pick up supplies he couldn't find in his town. He'd mentioned he might come back and I asked if he'd bring me a sweater I'd left at his place. It was uncanny but I *knew* he was close. I could *feel* him.

Later that day, after dropping my daughter at soccer practice, I let my grief pour out. I cried to White Owl, saying, "I am so sorry. I am back to 'Daughter Who Longs.' I can't help it. Please make me strong. Please help me through this."

Once again I reached out for Amelia, and her calm voice answered the phone. All I had to say through the tears was, "I'm back to Daughter Who Longs," and she knew exactly where I was. She recommended a homeopathic that she said would work for acute grief called Ignatia. She told me to take 200 ccs of it a few times a day, saying it would help with the emotions that stemmed from the core wound. I made my way to our organic market and picked up the medicine.

The following day, while kneeling in front of my altar, talking to White Owl, I fell into sobbing and begging. I feel embarrassment sharing this—but this is where I was. I was deep in the wound at this time of my life and that was clearly where I was meant to be until I could navigate my way through.

I begged White Owl, "Please, sister. Please. Please. Please. Make him want to see me. Please let him call me. Please don't let him go back home without seeing me. Please let him come to me in love." I realize that to some I sound pathetic. But this was my process, and rather than numb myself on antidepressants, which I abhor, I chose to feel everything.

The following day Leif did call, saying he'd been in town a couple of days. He said he had my sweater and asked if I wanted to meet him that afternoon. We met at a park and spent an hour walking his dog and talking. When we parted, he held me, squeezed my body tightly into his, and kissed me deeply.

We were supposed to go to Belize together for ten days the following month. The trip was already paid for and we were to stay at a very special jungle lodge. The lodge sat next to a beautiful river, and I felt her (the river) call to me when I was on my last medicine journey. There were significant Mayan ruins nearby as well as the healing center of a medicine woman, Rosita Arvigo. I had read her books and I very much wanted to meet her.

I felt excitement about every aspect of the Belize trip, but I had trepidation about going with Leif. I didn't know what to expect. I was hopeful we could re-establish our connection, but nothing was certain.

I decided at this point to turn it over to White Owl. She was my guardian. I was in personal crisis and this was an opportunity to go very deeply into her medicine with total dedication and trust. I felt that my current life situation was no accident. It was all serving to ultimately bring me to my power. And I realized that the way to my power was through *absolute surrender*.

I knelt in front of my altar once again, holding my white owl fan, and said, "Sister White Owl, I will stop trying to control my life. I surrender. I can only do what I can do. I cannot make other people do what I want them to. I am not a sorcerer. I will not ask you to make someone want me. I surrender to you. I am your servant in the beauty way. I ask that you lend me your support so I can take care of my girls when we move out of here. I will give of myself and I will honor your beautiful energies. I will teach and offer healing to others. I will open myself to bring through your grace with humility and reverence. I surrender. I surrender."

Almost immediately after doing so, things began to shift for me. I surrendered daily to White Owl. I endeavored simply to walk the beauty way. I reminded myself throughout the day, "I am Daughter Who Knows." And I babied myself with good food, exercise, and lots of sleep.

One of my regular clients, Leah, came to see me for an appointment, announcing she had a gift for me. Expressing her gratitude for everything I had done for her over the years, she proceeded to write me a check for a thousand dollars! I was beside myself. This was money I really needed and it was being gifted to me with incredible kindness and generosity. In that moment, I felt White Owl's presence around me and I knew I was being supported.

The following day, I received a check from someone who owed me a few hundred dollars. I had figured I wouldn't see that money for a good while but it showed up, completely unexpected.

A day later I spoke with Leif and his warmth and accessibility was a welcome balm. We discussed the trip to Belize, both of us anxious to get away to bright sunshine and heat. I was past my neediness at this point—my intention was to simply be in the moment. There was ease to the conversation that hadn't been there in over a month. I felt levity within myself that I hadn't thought was possible.

When I hung up, I felt the longing creep in and I immediately knelt before my altar, asking White Owl to fill the void. I stayed like that for several minutes, meditating on the healing of my core wound. When it felt complete, the feeling of emptiness was gone.

I had found my way to a most beautiful expression of Spirit in the form of White Owl. Through my connection to her, and my daily practice of surrender, I was healing myself. I chose to walk in beauty, and my life began to shift in wondrous ways.

~ 17 ~

Snakebite and a Healing

Education is very important. People need to understand that snakes are not out to bite them and prefer to be left alone. They should realize that it is not their duty or right to kill snakes out of hand. Being a snake is not a crime and even venomous snakes serve a valuable purpose by acting as a natural control of disease-carrying, rice stealing rodents.
—Mark O'Shea, *Venomous Snakes of the World*

I had an intuitive sense that Belize was going to be an extraordinary trip. I felt called to be there and by now I was feeling very good about where I was emotionally and spiritually. I had experienced my own personal descent of Inanna that felt almost choreographed. It seemed to be a requisite initiation of clearing, cleansing, and healing before my trip to the rich jungles of Belize.

The airport taxi picked me up and then headed over to get Leif. Once inside the cab, he pulled me close and kissed me like he meant it. I felt our connection restored, and at the same time, I felt myself as grounded and centered. We were off to a good start.

We arrived in Belize and were picked up at the airport by one of the friendly guides from the lodge where we'd be staying. It was a two-and-a-half-hour drive to our destination and we arrived at nightfall. We were shown to cabin number six and I smiled when I saw the number. I am always exploring the symbolism of numbers. Six is the Lovers card in the Tarot. I gave the spirits a nod and said silently, "Nice touch."

We spent the first couple of days acclimating to our new surroundings. We were to stay ten days at this place. Unlike the other guests who would embark daily on the numerous day-trips offered, we chose to stay mostly at the lodge exploring the surrounding jungle. It was a luxury to simply take our time and get to know the place.

Toward the end of our second day, Leif and I swam across the Macal River to a trail leading upward to a summit with a gorgeous view. We stayed at the top for a while and then made our way down. It was almost six o'clock and close to getting dark. Turning a corner, I saw the most beautiful red and black snake slithering off the trail. I am a lover of those creatures and I often catch and hold the garter snakes that live on my land. Without thinking, I saw only the opportunity to catch it. I foolishly caught it up in my hands to admire it. Then it bit me.

Sharp fangs sliced into my right ring finger and I realized in horror that I had just picked up a snake in the middle of the jungle in Central America. No one in his right mind would do such a thing, but I was not thinking in that moment; it all happened so fast. I dropped the snake, saying, "It bit me," then hightailed it to the bottom of the trail where I jumped into the river to swim to the other side to get help.

Leif wasn't convinced it was anything to worry about, but as soon as those fangs pierced my finger I knew it was venomous. When I got to the main office and announced I'd been bitten, they went into high gear.

They sat me down with a towel and asked what color the snake was. I told them it was red and black and they asked quickly, "Was there any yellow?" I said, "No." and they asked if I was absolutely sure.

They have a saying that goes, "Red and yellow, kill a fellow. Red and black, stay back." Fortunately for me, there was no yellow on that snake, but it was still a venomous bite and the pain in my finger was increasing, coming in waves. By now I was scared and in shock. I found out days later that I'd had a conversation with one of the guides while in the office, but I don't remember him being there.

One of the managers of the lodge, Giovanni, told me he would be taking me to the hospital. I ran to our room, where I took a lightning-fast shower. Leif helped me dress and we rushed to the waiting car. It was about forty-five minutes into the town of San Ignacio, where there was a little hospital. The road out of the lodge was nothing but potholes and the ride was crazy. By now the pain was excruciating and was travelling up my arm. I could feel stiffness in my elbow joint and that frightened me.

When I am in trouble like this I go into cat mode, which is to say that I stay relatively quiet and try not to draw a lot of attention to myself. I was actually in good spirits in the car and I felt very bad for ruining everyone's night with my foolishness. Giovanni was in high spirits, impressed with my good nature and intent on reassuring me and making sure I got the best care.

We reached a small, darkened hospital and I swear to God we had to knock on a door! The doctor and nurses were very nice but they did not want to administer anti-venom without knowing what kind of snake bit me. By now I was feeling a tightening in my chest area in addition to the excruciating waves of pain pulsating from my finger.

At this point I got very scared. I silently prayed to Spirit saying, "Please. I know I did a stupid thing, but I have my two girls and I don't want to die yet. Please hear me." It wasn't until a few weeks later that I received a message from Spirit that Archangel Michael was in the room with me. I was given a vision of a radiant angel hovering just behind my head.

The doctor chose to shoot me up with more painkillers, which did nothing. I was sent to a larger hospital in Belize City, ninety minutes away. At the next hospital, I was shown to a little room where I was hooked up to an I.V. and administered the anti-venom. No amount of painkiller had any effect, but once the anti-venom was given, the pain receded in a couple of hours. Giovanni left to spend the night with a friend in town and Leif stayed with me in my room. He was caring and sweet and he stayed by my side the whole time.

The following morning Giovanni returned to check on me. They were threatening to keep me another night but I was having none of it. I would have to stay till noon for blood tests to be complete but I was determined to leave after that. Giovanni suggested taking Leif for an outing and I insisted they go. I felt bad enough for ruining our night; I did not want Leif to be stuck in a hospital room with me for the next four hours.

After they left, two of the nurses came in and we started talking. They were intrigued with me—the crazy white woman who'd picked up a snake in the jungle. They told me how lucky I was to be alive and then they said that I had a very good man. They were impressed by how attentive Leif had been. Unfortunately for Central and

South American women, their men are not always the most loyal or reliable. One of the nurses, Louisa, began telling me the sad story of her man.

She had a husband who was less than faithful to her. She confessed that when she caught him cheating, she would beat him silly, and said that she actually had to go to counseling for it. I was struck by how casually she revealed this to me, with no self-consciousness, just a frank reporting. She added that he would sometimes beat her too. My heart ached for the violence she so willingly accepted as her lot in life.

She continued by saying that she had a neighbor woman who had four kids from four different men. This woman became obsessed with Louisa's husband and paid a sorcerer to put an enchantment on him so he would fall in love with her. He began spending time at this neighbor's house, and when he came home to Louisa, the woman would text her, tormenting her with lewd details of what she'd done to him in bed.

Her husband was now living with that woman. He'd walked out on her and their three kids and was shacked up with the whore, as Louisa called her. To make matters worse, the whore had put a curse on Louisa and her home. Putting curses on people or things is very common in these cultures.

So is the use of sorcerers, who work with black magic with deleterious results for those on the receiving end. I was blessed to have learned curse unraveling from a master shaman in my area. When I told Louisa I was a shaman, she was all ears. Louisa was working so I could not do a formal unraveling, but I did share with her what she could do on her own to dissolve the curse and empower herself.

I told her about my work with women and my desire to see them empowered. We talked about being women and Louisa said two things that I will never forget. As she reflected on the difficult times she'd had in her life she said proudly, "I take my lickins like a WOMAN." I loved that! She didn't take her lickins like a man. She took them like a WOMAN. As if it were obvious how strong a woman is. She continued, "A woman is like a teabag. You don't know her strength till she's in hot water."

I fell in love with Louisa in that moment. She was a hard-working woman with three kids to support and no man to love and help her. She was no stranger to violence and hard times. Yet she had pride and strength that I admired greatly. I hoped I had given her some good tools to shift the energy in her home and take her power back. I was getting that this snakebite incident was no accident. I knew our conversation was meant to happen.

By noon I was told I could leave the hospital. Giovanni and Leif returned, ebullient. They had taken a ten-minute flight to Caye Caulker, a tiny island off the coast of Belize, where Leif had swum in the salt water. They'd had a delicious lunch and were feeling rejuvenated. I was very happy to hear it. I hoped it made up for our less than luxurious night in the hospital.

We returned to the lodge late Sunday afternoon. That night, exhausted from three nights of little sleep, we fell into a deep slumber, awaking on Monday well rested. I was happy to be alive and Leif was happy I was still around. At one point he pulled me to him and said, "Christ, Shonagh! You could have died. And you have those girls. Thank God you're all right." He'd been so calm throughout the whole thing, but in that moment I felt his relief.

At breakfast, which was taken in a gorgeous thatch-roofed common area that was open to the jungle and the Macal River below, Giovanni came to us smiling like a cat. I had mentioned to him when we first arrived that I wanted to meet Rosita Arvigo. She apprenticed for thirteen years with Mayan shaman, Don Elijio Panti, who passed away a few years earlier. She was a healer, teacher, and author whom I had admired for a number of years.

On the flight to Belize, I read Arvigo's book, *Sastun*, for the second time. I figured since we were going to be staying so close to where she was, I might as well have her story fresh in my mind. Our lodge sat across from the Elijio Panti National Park and I knew Rosita lived close by. Giovanni told us that she just happened to be giving a talk that night at a nearby lodge. We would get a lift later in the day and I would have my chance to finally meet her.

That evening, I found myself sitting in a room with a group of people, listening to Rosita tell the story of her time with Don Elijio. In the front row were five women who had arrived with Rosita. They were obviously her students and they all wore little medicine bags around their necks. I felt a desire within to be one of those students. I can tune into people pretty well and I felt Rosita's integrity immediately.

When she finished her talk, a number of people went up to meet her. I waited for my chance and then said to her, "Rosita, I want you to know that I have read your books and have admired you for some time now. In fact, I mentioned you in a book I wrote called, *Ix Chel Wisdom* . . ." Before I could finish the title she finished it for me. "*Seven Teachings from the Mayan Sacred Feminine!* I read your book! One of my students gifted it to me and I loved it!" I was absolutely floored and I almost wept, I was so humbled by her words.

Rosita then turned to her students and said, "Guess who's here? Shonagh Home! The author of *Ix Chel*

Wisdom!" Her students lit up. They clearly knew of my book. I was shocked and very touched by their enthusiasm. They were so friendly. I wanted to stay there and learn from all of them.

I told Rosita we were staying nearby and then I told her about my snakebite. I felt rather foolish telling her that I had picked up a snake in the jungle. I explained that my love of the serpents overrode my common sense, to which she replied, smiling, "You're human!"

I don't know what I expected her to say, but I was certain she would chastise me just a little. Her lack of judgment and her genuine warmth and kindness was a healing for me. In that moment I became aware of my own harsh self-judgment. I'd been feeling like an idiot for my foolishness. Here was this beautiful *curandera*, whose home was the jungle, responding to me with pure compassion and understanding. I decided right there that someday soon, I would study with her.

Rosita then examined my finger and told me it was still hot and would need to release the poison. She told me to find a plant called snake plant and cut off the top four or five inches. I was to then mash it in a bowl with a pinch of salt and then put the mash around my finger, securing it with plastic and a Band-Aid. That would draw out the remaining poison and the finger would heal.

This was my kind of medicine. This is medicine that has been passed down for generations and it's still around because it works. Rosita also spoke about spiritual illness, caused by unresolved emotional stress and distress. Don Elijio taught her eighteen different pulses that indicated eighteen different spiritual illnesses. There was a Mayan prayer for each specific illness and these prayers worked. I felt quickened by the information she was sharing and I put out my intention to travel back the following year to take her Spiritual Healing course.

Leif took photos of Rosita and me and we made our way back to our home away from home. I was struck as always by the seamlessness of events. Synchronicity was at play, and I opened myself in total trust to whatever Spirit had in mind for me.

18

Jungle Spirits

*As I sat, I had the sensation that something was moving
through my body down into the earth. It was as if a zipper
ran through my flesh, and some of my energy was being
absorbed by the ground beneath me. For that moment,
there was peace within and peace without. I felt welcomed
by the Spirits, grateful and humbled by the love around me.*
—Rosita Arvigo, Nadine Epstein, *Spiritual Bathing*

On one of our exploratory hikes through the jungle,
Leif and I found an enchanted stream. It was about
a half-hour walk from our cabin along a gorgeous path
of green. You could feel the shift in the energy when you
came upon it. The stream was a series of graduating pools,
each filled with tiny black snails. This delighted Leif, as he
was a huge fan of the mollusks. The rock formations that
had formed between each pool of water looked like skilled
hands had sculpted them. The vegetation was lush with
tall trees draped in vines and ferns of every size.

I had wanted to do a formal Mayan ceremony to
engage the spirits as well as apologize to the snake people. I realized that I had picked up that snake without
asking permission—very rude. We decided we would do

ceremony in this beautiful place. We would also take a light dose of the mushroom medicine, enough to open the portal and engage the nature spirits.

At the entrance to the stream, I set up my altar in front of a small tree. I brought with me offerings of cacao beans, bee pollen, and tiny colored stones from my altar at home. I placed cards from a Mayan oracle deck on the altar that bore images of specific Mayan deities like Ix Chel, Lord Pacal, the jaguar, etc. Our mushroom medicine was also there to be blessed before we took it.

I opened the directions and gave my offerings, asking for protection and guidance from the spirits. Then I made a formal apology to the snake people. We took the medicine and then packed up the altar to make our way up the stream. We waded along the pools, careful not to step on any snails, and found our way to a place where we could sit on dry rock. I sat by the base of a tree facing the graduating pools and I was immediately captivated by a large portion of jungle farther ahead in the center of the stream.

I focused my attention there and expanded my energy field to meld with the beautiful surroundings. At some point an eye appeared and regarded me. I opened my heart to it and sent it my light. It stayed for a few minutes and then receded. It was followed by a number of nature spirits, who would appear for a few minutes to regard me curiously and then recede. The last spirit to appear was the snake wearing a vertical crown. I took the opportunity to say simply, "I'm very sorry."

"All is forgiven. Learn the medicine," it replied.

Then a ray of sun shone diagonally through the cluster of jungle foliage. Inside the ray were nine bright lights. I knew they were Mayan spirits. Again, I opened my heart and sent them my light. The area had a very soft, feminine feel. I let myself sink into the sweetness of the energy.

At the same time, Leif had discovered the most beautiful green and red frog. It was in the pool beneath him and it actually chirped at him. Frogs come to both Leif and me, although Leif is particularly enamored of them. He was thrilling on this little guy that eventually made its way into the foliage on the edge of the pond. It was hiding but we could see him expertly blending in with the green leaves.

I spoke silently to the spirits, saying of Leif, "See how beautiful he is? Can you feel how reverent he is around your little beings? This is why I love him so much."

Gazing into the jungle, I realized to my amazement that the water from the upper pool that was flowing over a rock formation into the pond just in front of me was in the exact shape of Pan's face. The water flowing from the right and left side of the rock formed the two horns. The two streams of flowing water met at the center and flowed over a rock face creating a spitting image of Pan. I cried out in excitement, "There's Pan!" Leif saw it too and snapped a couple of photos. Sure enough, when we checked the pictures later, you could see Pan's face very clearly.

Pan is an ever-present spirit for me and I was thrilled that he had made himself visible to us again. A few minutes later the jungle spirits spoke to me and said, "No one comes to honor us in this way. You are the first." I smiled my love to them.

"Do you have a wish?" they asked.

"I wish for you to always be green. I wish for you vitality and vibrancy. I wish for you abundance of your beautiful trees and foliage." I radiated my gratitude and appreciation to the spirits and I felt myself being blessed.

Leif and I stood up, taking in our surroundings. He stepped over the rocks and took me in his arms, hugging me close. We stood like this for several minutes, holding each other within our tranquil jungle sanctuary. Then we stood apart, to gaze at the lush vegetation all around us. I had a surreal moment pass over me where I felt us as the lord and lady of the stream. It was so real. It was as if the masculine and feminine energy of the stream flowed through us and we simply stood regally, taking in its beauty.

After a few minutes the sensation passed, but I could not shake the feeling that something had come into me, giving me a glimpse into a very different realm. What I found especially interesting was that as soon as we began to make our way back down the stream, the energy shifted. I realized we'd tapped into a portal in that specific part of the stream and I could feel the difference as we moved away from the area. Both of us were so taken by the place that we made a plan to return once more before we left for home.

Throughout the week we continued to explore the jungle, horseback riding, caving, and swimming in the Macal River. There was a relaxed camaraderie between us and it was clear we were good travel companions. We spent most of our time away from the other hotel guests, content to be in each other's company, immersed in nature.

Later in the week we decided to take a day trip to Pine Mountain Forest, to explore a large cave and swim at a place called Big Rock Falls. Our guide was a young man named Merell with whom we had a nice connection. It was a two-hour drive to our destination and I sat in the front of the car chatting with him.

Merell felt very at ease talking with us and eventually the topic of shamanism came up. He confided a story about a curse his grandfather had put on the whole family many years ago. He said there had been bad luck for them ever since. He then told us that just a week ago, his aunt had come to his house and unleashed her anger over a family matter. She then insulted his deceased mother and put a curse on him.

Merell is a quiet man who prefers to keep to himself. His nature is gentle and he was visibly upset by what he felt was an unprovoked attack. Leif volunteered my services, assuring him I could take care of the curses. Remembering my earlier conversation with Louisa, I was struck at how ingrained cursing is within these cultures.

Curses have been used by every culture around the world. They have the power to throw a person off balance and negatively affect them on a number of levels. This imprints the psyche with a belief that is completely out of alignment with the truth of the individual. We underestimate the power and energy of words. When words are combined with intense emotion, the energy sends those words directly into the psyche of the person on the receiving end. This can bind the person to the words, disrupting their life on many levels.

If a sorcerer activates a curse, it carries even more power. A sorcerer is working in conjunction with various spirit energies that empower the curse. People in the West dismiss this kind of thing, saying it doesn't work if you don't believe it. In cultures where this is prevalent, a sorcerer's curse is not to be underestimated. The unfortunate individual will usually find a good shaman to undo the curse, sometimes asking the shaman to send a curse off to the original source. A good shaman will not go there.

My intention for Merell was to go into the nature of the curses and restore his energy back to him. I would empower him through ritual, which would free him from carrying the burden of the curse.

When we entered the mouth of the cave, I knew it was the right place to do the unraveling. It was a large cave with a beautiful pool of crystalline water. There were boulders one could clamber over to explore the areas on the other side. I found a sandy place that was situated behind some rocks next to a clear pool of water. It was private and quiet. I went to the water to submerge my hands and ask to be cleared and cleansed before I did the ritual. In the water I found a thick wooden stick that resembled a wand. I held it in my hands and decided to use it in the ritual. I felt it carried the energies of the water and the cave. I asked the spirit within the stick if I could work with it. I got a "yes" and I called Merell over to begin.

I had him lie on the ground and proceeded to prepare the space around us energetically. Then I called in my animal guardian that I work with for curse unraveling, which happens to be the snake. I explained that I would work with the curse from the aunt, and then work on the grandfather's curse. The family curse from the grandfather felt like it carried more weight for him.

As I worked with the first curse, I felt that his heart carried the wound of his aunt's angry words. I placed a comforting hand on his arm to connect us and placed my right hand over his heart, returning his energy and sending in healing. When I felt it was complete, I tuned in to the older curse from the grandfather. Energetically, I could feel intense bitterness and anger around the old curse. I worked with my spirit animal and did the unraveling, returning to each party the energy they had put into it.

I focused this part of the healing on Merell's third chakra, his power center, as this curse was about disempowering others. I placed my right hand over his third chakra and channeled through a healing. When I was done I picked up the "wand" I found and shook it over him like a rattle, working with the spirit to bless and protect him, sealing in the work.

When we were finished, Merell looked totally different, as if a great weight had been lifted. He was surprised by how much energy he felt coming from my hands. I told him everything I experienced during the ritual and assured him that the energy of the curses had been unwound. I gave him some tips for keeping himself protected and he thanked me sincerely. He was genuinely grateful and I sent up my own prayer of thanks for the opportunity to serve another in the spirit of compassion and love.

Finally, I gave him the stick I'd used as a wand. He held it reverently and decided to hide it in a secret place inside the cave. He said he would come back there later and use it for his own rituals. It was a good gesture of sharing magic and it completed the ritual beautifully.

On our last day in Belize we took the morning to visit a nearby Mayan site. Our guide just happened to be a young man who descended from a line of Mayan medicine men. He knew everything about the plants all around us and led me to another plant that could treat my snakebite. Because of his background, he was very supportive of my desire to do a ceremony at the site and pay my respects to the spirits.

When we returned it was early afternoon. We rested for a while and then made our way once again to our beautiful stream. We were tired, but I wanted to do the medicine one last time. The following day we would leave that place forever and I couldn't miss one last opportunity to engage the spirits.

We made our way to the stream in the late afternoon. Once there, I did a simple ceremony with more offerings of cacao and bee pollen. I also brought a traditional dessert I'd purchased from a street vendor the day before. Spirits feed off the essence of an offering and I thought they'd appreciate this treat. We ingested a larger dose of medicine for this journey. If you take the medicine consistently, you build a tolerance to it. Normally, we would do a heroic dose with a period of recovery afterward. This was an exception to the rule as we only had so much time to dip into that well.

When I felt the medicine take hold, I lay on my back on the dry rock and said, "Sweet mama, sing me the jungle." I smiled blissfully as the leaves of the trees came to life. I was awash in gratitude for the privilege of being in such a sacred, beautiful place. I wanted to soak it up as much as I possibly could before returning to the grey gloom of Seattle winter.

At one point I heard the spirits saying over and over, "So honored. So honored." I sent out my heart's light in response. The journey was a soft, subtle experience where I bathed in the energy of the jungle and offered my gratitude for the privilege of being there.

A couple of hours later I felt the day waning and realized it would be dusk when we made our way home. For the first time that week, I felt a fear creep in. It was a fear of coming across another snake. They came out in the very early morning and at dusk. I did not want to experience another bite.

The minute I felt this fear, the spirits spoke to me, saying, "Daughter, do not fear. We will see you safely home.

The snake people will keep away." I believed them, and at the same time, I knew we had to make our way back. I let Leif know we needed to get going. He was enjoying his own exploration of the flora and fauna and was reluctant to leave. I gently prodded him and we slowly made our way down the path of the stream. We gingerly walked along the rock formations, ever aware of the delicate snails dotting the streambeds and stone.

I reached the entrance to the stream first and Leif was a bit behind me, taking pictures. While I waited for him, I noticed a large butterfly on the same tree I'd set my altar next to a few days earlier. I had specifically chosen that tree, feeling its invitation to set my sacred objects next to it. I stood still, admiring the butterfly when it gently lifted off the branch and flew in my direction. It alighted on my forehead, right between my eyes. It then lifted off and landed on my right shoulder, finally lifting off and landing on the branch of a tree just to the right of me.

I called to Leif softly and told him to come see it and take a picture. The butterfly stayed perfectly still and Leif took a few shots. We then began our walk home. I was walking a little faster and would have to stop and wait for Leif, who was savoring the beauty of the various jungle plants that would catch his eye. I was keeping my eye on the sky, trying to judge how much time we had left before darkness settled in.

A few minutes later I felt myself getting nervous. No sooner did it hit me than the butterfly appeared, flitting around me. The spirits then spoke to me and said, "Daughter, do not doubt. We told you we would see you home safely and it is so." I was surprised to see the butterfly again and I called Leif to check it out.

Love and Spirit Medicine

We continued on the path and I was lost in my own thoughts. I started to connect with the Mayan mother goddess, Ix Chel. No sooner had I thought the name, Ix Chel, than the butterfly appeared in that exact moment! I called to Leif again and this time it came to me that it was our guardian, sent to us by the spirits of the stream to see us home. Its appearances coincided with specific thoughts and feelings I was having. The spirits were making it as obvious as possible that they were with us.

It followed us most of the way home and at one point when it showed up, I put out my right hand and the butterfly immediately alighted upon it. I asked Leif to take a picture and the butterfly stayed on my hand for a couple of minutes, plenty of time for Leif to get a few good shots. This was no butterfly. This was a dear guardian spirit, and it was engaging me with such sweetness. It flitted all around us on our path of green, and time stood still in our enchanted jungle.

When we finally reached our cabin, it was just dark. The timing of it all was pure perfection. I said a silent thank-you and marveled at the magical experience we had just shared. I felt a message come in saying that "Our work here is done." I understood that to mean that our energetic signatures had melded with the energies of the jungle and the people we'd connected with. We had all been enriched in the most wondrous ways. It was time to go home and integrate these powerful experiences.

☞ 19 ☜

Snake Medicine/ Butterfly Medicine

Snakes or serpents were very early symbols of the Great Mother Goddesses. Serpents had dual spiritual meanings, even when shown singular: life and death, solar and lunar, good and evil, healing and poison. The snake was considered to be an embodiment of all potentials of a physical, material and spiritual nature.

—D.J. Conway, *Animal Magick*

Butterfly: Magickal Attributes: Reincarnation, magick, beauty, love. Transformation of the personality and life. Understanding where you are in the cycle of your life and using it to the fullest.

—D.J. Conway, *Animal Magick*

Coming home, I knew I needed to spend time exploring the medicine of these two sacred messengers that presented themselves so dramatically to me in Belize. In native cultures, animals have spiritual powers and are imbued with symbolic meanings. When a specific animal crosses your path, it is understood that it has great significance for you and an important message to impart.

Before beginning my research, I knew that both the snake and the butterfly were highly potent arbiters of transmutation and rebirth. They heralded great change and I was definitely in the throes of a major life transition.

In a few months, I would be leaving the cocoon of my comfortable home. I would be venturing out on my own, relying on my private practice, my teaching, and my writing to support my girls and myself. I was releasing a belief system I'd always carried that said I couldn't be on my own without a man to support me.

Strangely, I felt no sense of fear or panic around this. My relationship with Ix Chel, the Earth Mother, and White Owl, was grounded in trust. Too many synchronicities had occurred that cemented my faith that I was being guided and cared for by Spirit. My eyes were open and my intuitive functions were alert. I knew that as long as I walked the beauty way—surrendering to Spirit and doing my work with women—I would always be taken care of.

As I began my exploration on the snake, it was not lost on me that it had been a powerful symbol in ancient cultures of the feminine. The snake symbolizes wisdom, healing, initiation, and secret knowledge. It represents eternal life and the cycle of death and rebirth.

One of the things that struck me about the snake was how close to the Earth it lives. Its entire body slithers along the ground and it burrows deep into the Earth to hibernate. It felt like a metaphor for my deepening relationship to Mother Earth and my nightly ritual of sinking into her before I fell asleep. My first lesson was the importance of staying grounded and connected to the Earth.

In addition to being connected to the Earth, I knew that this was about burrowing deep within myself. It was about taking time away from the daily concerns to access the resources I carried beneath the surface. The snake embodies wisdom and higher knowledge, which is found deep within.

Then of course, there is the shedding of its skin. I was quite familiar with this because the snake is the guardian of the direction of the south in Peruvian shamanism. In the medicine-wheel training I teach, we begin with this direction, which is about shedding the past completely in order to make room for the new. One is shedding the old ways of being so they can move forward, unhindered by the past. I understood very clearly that I was releasing the skin of my old identity to bring forth a new self.

This shedding of the skin is the transmutation process that is the crux of snake medicine. It is not a small endeavor and cannot be underestimated. This is about major life change and the wisdom to know when to initiate it. The snake has an internal knowing that it relies on to determine when the transmutation process is to begin. This is significant. We must be connected to our own internal rhythms and wisdom, so that we know when it is time to let go.

If we stay the same we do not grow, we stagnate. The snake represents the necessary cycle of death and rebirth. It is a symbol of eternity as represented by the *ouroboros*, the snake swallowing its tail—no beginning and no end. We are eternal beings engaging in a constant cycle of death and rebirth. With rebirth comes higher wisdom.

By surrendering myself to Spirit every day, I had invited my own death in a way. I was not surrendering lightly. I was giving myself over completely. I was willing to give up everything to serve the Divine Mother. Here I was, about to leave my marriage, my home, my security, and my way of life for the past seven years—and I was not a young woman.

This is where I felt the full power of the snake medicine. The snake undergoes the process of transmutation so thoroughly that trust doesn't even enter the equation. It sheds its skin willingly and effortlessly, leaving behind the old and advancing forward renewed and unfettered.

Jamie Sams and David Carson have an excellent book called *Medicine Cards*. This passage jumped out at me: "The power of snake medicine is the power of creation, for it embodies sexuality, psychic energy, alchemy, reproduction and ascension (or immortality). The transmutation of the life-death-rebirth cycle is exemplified by the shedding of the snake's skin. It is the energy of wholeness, cosmic consciousness, and the ability to experience anything willingly and without resistance."

Flow was a necessity. Just as the snake moves with ease and grace, often with remarkable speed, I was doing the same, allowing the forces of change to propel me forward. I simply focused on cultivating my practice and my teaching, knowing that this is where my focus needed to be.

In terms of transmuting poison, I thought of my response to the painful experience I had with Leif in December. Rather than go into victim, I went deep into the pain of it and accessed a strength and wisdom I didn't know I had. It made me think of the old saying, "That which doesn't kill you will make you stronger." When we take on the poison of a difficult experience, either we let it sicken us or we shift our perspective around it, thereby accessing the gift that can be found through adversity.

Another aspect of snake medicine is its relationship to the creative life-force energy known as kundalini Shakti. Kundalini means coiled and Shakti means power. The kundalini resides in the base of the spine and is represented by a coiled serpent. It's activated when we engage in spiritual practices like meditation, yoga, shamanism, etc. Once activated, the kundalini will begin to rise up the spine, enervating our chakras along the way and infusing them with its potent life-force energy. This greatly expands our consciousness and can lead to profound spiritual awakening.

My kundalini had been reactivated on the mushroom medicine. My sense was that the snake was also a harbinger of more activity in this area as well. Over the past few months, I had been experiencing more pulsating waves of energy when I lay in bed at night. My intuition told me there was more to come with this energy in the near future.

I understood that multiple layers of my existence were undergoing this intense transmutation process. I felt the full weight of the power of snake medicine. It is not subtle. My piece was to stay out of resistance and allow the process to continue to its completion.

Knowing the snake was a symbol of the feminine sealed my trust that all was in the hands of the Divine Mother. I chose not to limit the outcome with any fears or expectations of what my future would hold. And I looked to the butterfly for further guidance.

When I reviewed the many photos Leif had taken of our trip to Belize, I was struck by how many of them had me wearing a butterfly necklace I'd brought with me. It wasn't until the butterfly presented itself to me so dramatically that I began to explore its powerful medicine.

There is no greater symbol of metamorphosis and transformation than the butterfly. It's about moving from one phase of life to another and accessing new heights. The butterfly has freed itself from the container of the cocoon, to live the full expression of its being. It is a symbol of joy in motion.

Butterfly medicine takes you from the physical realm upward to the spiritual realms. It's associated with the element of air, which rules the mind and higher order thinking. The butterfly symbolizes expanded awareness, drawing us upward into the higher realms of consciousness.

In his book, *Experience and Philosophy*, Franklin Merrell-Wolff devotes a chapter to this creature called "The Symbolism of the Butterfly." In this chapter he writes, "The butterfly consciousness has certain very clear advantages. The butterfly, as compared to the caterpillar, moves in a world of an infinitely vaster comprehension. It lives in space with the power to return to surfaces. It is thus in a position to understand surface relationships, the whole domain of the caterpillar, but, in addition, knows an infinitely richer world that is utterly unknown to the caterpillar. Further, it knows surfaces in relation to depth, and thus can master problems connected with surfaces that quite transcend the capacities of the caterpillar."

The cocoon is an important aspect of butterfly medicine. It serves as the alchemical container for transformation to occur. In the cocoon, the caterpillar dissolves, which can be a metaphor for the necessary annihilation of the old self during profound transitional life stages. These life stages are usually some form of dark night of the soul, which is a personal crisis that is all encompassing. The dark night of the soul is followed by transcendence and spiritual illumination. The butterfly can only survive if it completes the process of transformation within the cocoon. If we try to hasten its exit, it will not be able to fly. There is no hastening a dark night of the soul, either. One must navigate through it and release one's attachments to the old way of being.

There is great wisdom in knowing when the time is right to leave the cocoon. When that time comes, the butterfly inspires us to spread our wings and let go entirely. We must be willing to be vulnerable and trusting in the rebirth process. This is the opportunity to unleash the expression of our beauty on a higher level, after the alchemical forces have worked their magic.

There is levity and joy to the butterfly, which are aspects of the medicine I am sometimes in need of. I tend to get weighted down with my concerns to the point that I deny myself the opportunity to taste the sweetness of life. These aspects of the butterfly suggest that change can be a positive experience rather than traumatic. If we can stay out of resistance and attachment, change can be a gentle, joyful process.

Another important piece of butterfly medicine is courage. When we leave the safety of the cocoon it requires courage to spread our wings and fly into a whole new experience. Transformation brings expanded possibilities and a higher perspective. With courage, we can take those first few steps and bring ourselves into the full expression of our potential.

Both creatures were teaching exactly the wisdom needed. There couldn't have been two better messengers to assist me at this time of my life than the snake and the butterfly. I put representations of them on my altar as a way of honoring them and deepening into their medicine. I would meditate on them daily to further my connection and integrate their wisdom.

⁀ 20 ⁀

The Beginning of the End

*Someday you're gonna look back at this moment of your
life as such a sweet time of grieving. You'll see that you were
in mourning and your heart was broken, but your life was
changing . . .*

—Elizabeth Gilbert, *Eat Pray Love*

Upon returning, it was clear that my relationship with
Leif was not resolved either way. Belize had been a
great trip and we'd gotten along well, but it was rather
superficial in that we never discussed our relationship or
what had happened in December. We were passionate
with each other but I felt his distance. I just didn't want
to acknowledge it.

We saw each other briefly the first week back and I let
him know that I would not be able to visit him for over
a month. He seemed disinterested and replied that he'd
have to check his plans before we solidified anything. He
left for home the following day and no call or email came
for over a week.

The following weekend my girls left to spend time
with their father. I took advantage of the quiet house and
immersed myself in my writing. Saturday evening I called

Leif but got his answering machine. Sunday morning he returned my call, and when I asked him where he'd been for over a week, he replied casually, "Right here." That stung. I couldn't help feeling a little hurt that he'd chosen not to contact me even briefly.

Later that afternoon I'd completed all the writing I could do. I gave in to my loneliness and knelt before my altar for another good cry. I thought about calling Leif again but I was afraid of coming off as needy. Then I thought, *Hell, if I can't call him when I'm lonely, then what is this?*

I dialed his number and got his answering machine. I left a message saying I was lonely and wanted to hear his voice. By nine-thirty that evening there was no return call. I decided to call him again. The answering machine picked up and I told him I had a lot on my mind and wanted to talk. I said he could call me as late as he wanted.

No call came until Monday afternoon. I was irritated, but he seemed sincere on the phone and wanted to know what was up. We talked for a while and then said goodbye. I hung up knowing our connection was weak at best. If I was going to be in a relationship with a man, I wanted to know we were close friends. How could I feel connected to Leif when we were barely communicating?

I contacted him a few days later to say that the dates I was planning to visit in April fell on the weekend of my daughter's school play. I asked if we could postpone until the following weekend, to which he replied, "Oh. I was planning on driving to California that weekend."

My first thought was, *Why didn't I know that? Why doesn't he talk to me about this stuff?* I replied that I would work around his schedule, but he didn't sound enthusiastic.

The conversation was stilted and I finally said, "I'm wondering if you even want me around."

"I'm just thawing out here," he responded.

"Ball's in your court, Leif. Talk to you later."

He said good-bye and hung up. Now I was pissed. *Finally.*

I wondered how much longer I could stay with a man who retreats so dramatically. It leaves room for a thousand assumptions on my part. All my insecurities were triggered and I was getting a big teaching on my own unresolved stuff. I was pissed *and* I didn't know what was really going on. He was a hermit. He craved his solitude. I knew this from the start of our relationship but I had chosen to stay. He had just spent eleven days with me and he wanted his space back. I should have left it at that, but I could not help thinking he didn't want me anymore. I certainly wasn't feeling any of the enthusiasm he'd had for me in the fall.

Later that night I let my assumptions win. I sent him a brief email that asked if he would send back a large kitchen knife I'd left in his knife rack. And I asked him to please include the gold ring I'd given him. I wrote out my address with a simple "thank you."

I was struck by the symbolism of these two items I'd requested. On the December mushroom journey I received a vision of a lifetime I'd experienced with Leif, and it was so powerfully intense and disturbing I never shared it with him. In that lifetime I saw myself on the sacrificial slab. I had been drugged so I could not move, but I was cognizant of what was happening. Leif was a high priest standing over me. He raised his knife and cut out my heart. It was still beating as he lifted it out of my body.

Back in January, in the thick of my anguish I'd thought about that. Whether it was a lifetime or a powerful metaphor, it was an interesting piece for my deep psyche to bring forward. In that "lifetime" I felt that he'd cut out my heart and sent me into death, which is the ultimate transformation. In this lifetime, I'd again given myself to him, only to have my heart broken or "cut out" in December. That sent me into a profound journey of transformation, this time on the Earth plane.

How interesting that I would be requesting back my large and very sharp knife. The knife felt like a symbol of my power that I had given away. I let myself get attached, and in so doing, got my heart cut out. Now I was requesting the knife back. I was taking back my power. The gold ring was a symbol of my love, which I didn't think he really wanted.

My astrologist friend, Alisha, had told me months earlier that soul-mate relationships are no walk in the park. She said soul mates come together for deep transformation and it can be very intense and heart wrenching. I knew through all my heartache that Leif and I were activating each other in ways that would no doubt offer us a deeper understanding of ourselves. However, it was indeed an excruciating process.

I then found a quote by Elizabeth Gilbert from her book, *Eat Pray Love*, which captured this so perfectly, it pained me to read it: "People think a soul mate is your perfect fit, and that's what everyone wants. But a true soul mate is a mirror, the person who shows you everything that is holding you back, the person who brings you to your own attention so you can change your life. A true soul mate is probably the most important person you'll ever meet, because they tear down your walls and smack you awake. But to live with a soul mate forever? Nah. Too painful. Soul mates, they come into your life just to reveal another layer of yourself to you, and then leave. A soul mate's purpose is to shake you up, tear apart your ego a little bit, show you your obstacles and addictions, break your heart open so new light can get in, make you so desperate and out of control that you have to transform your life."

I knew I had to let him go. I was way too attached and my pain was acute. A conversation with him would need to happen. I would have to initiate it, as he didn't seem to want to. I realized I'd have to dissolve the energetic cords that connect us. My friend, Amelia, was adept at that kind of healing and I made a note to call her. The time had come to let go of my attachment to him. I'd been crying over him for almost three months now. It was time to pull myself together.

I was sensing big change around the corner. The Spring Equinox was less than a week away. I was hosting an Equinox Ceremony and would be welcoming back Persephone from the underworld. I had identified with her archetype on the medicine back in December. I'd reread the Greek myth and knew that I had been on my own underworld journey for the past three months.

Letting go of my attachment to Leif would be the final piece to this. Spring was to herald a rebirth for me where I would come into a place of love and appreciation for the beautiful being that "I" was. I planned to use the energies of spring for regeneration—to fuel my forward movement toward *my* personal happiness. This was about loving myself enough not to have to look for it outside of me. If it came, I wanted to be in a place to receive it without needing it to define me.

I had Leif to thank for this. He was a powerful teacher for me. Leif was the catalyst that helped me end my dead marriage. He introduced me to the mushroom medicine, which has sent my life on a wondrous trajectory. He became the catalyst that brought me into my deepest wound, initiating a necessary process of healing and reflection. I would always be grateful to him for that.

I had opened to Leif so deeply, it took me into places of profound transformation. I still had pain and longing for him and I understood that this was my attachment to the cords that connected us. I felt there was a cord of love between us *and* there were dysfunctional cords that I had put forth which represented my grasping, needy aspects. It was these dysfunctional cords that I would be dissolving with Amelia. They were draining Leif and triggering me.

I would be doing the medicine with Amelia in just a few days. I chose to wait until after that event before talking to Leif. I didn't want to do the medicine with a heavy heart. I knew I had to release him. My desire for connection was putting a strain on Leif and his desire for solitude was crushing me.

How ironic. I was back to the Imago work. I had chosen someone once again who could not provide the one thing I craved—connection. My wound had been activated more profoundly with Leif than with anyone else because we had opened ourselves so deeply with the medicine.

I loved him, and . . . I wasn't doing either of us any favors by clinging to what we'd shared in the fall. If I let go of him I could create the space for both of us to return to each other, if we chose, from a whole new frame of reference. And if we chose not to return to each other, there would be space within each of us to welcome in what life wanted to offer. Attachment and neediness do not make for a healthy relationship. I had more work to do around this and it was my firm resolve to get myself to a centered place of self-love and self-nurturing. Only from that place would I be able to greet intimacy with another.

⇜ 21 ⇝

Shadow and Love

The psychic changes and unusual states of consciousness induced by hallucinogens are so far removed from similarity with ordinary life that it is scarcely possible to describe them in the language of daily living. A person under the effects of a hallucinogen forsakes his familiar world and operates under other standards, in strange dimensions and in a different time.

—Richard Evans Shultes, Albert Hofmann, and
Christian Ratsch, *Plants of the Gods: Their Sacred
Healing and Hallucinogenic Powers*

The day of our journey, I decided on a whim to look up the butterflies of Belize. I was curious to see what kind of butterfly had followed me back on the trail that last night in the jungle. The photo of my magic butterfly had been added to my website and also my Facebook homepage. I was feeling its presence, as I was acutely aware of being in the chrysalis. I Googled "butterflies of Belize" and found a page with several pictures of them. I scrolled down and found its photo and to my utter astonishment, read the name:

Owl Butterfly.

My whole body began to shake. What were the odds? I was rocked by this discovery. The veils were coming down around me. Never before had I felt the spirits so palpably in my life. I had engaged them with the intention of being in service to life. I was consistent and sincere and now here they were, responding with absolute magic and love.

When Amelia arrived, I told her the story and she too was amazed. We took that as an auspicious sign and got ourselves ready to begin the medicine ceremony. I smudged the room and each of us with sage, using the white owl fan. I called in White Owl for her protection and guidance and we sat on our cozy beds and ate the mushrooms.

The medicine kicked in about a half hour later and hit me hard. I knew immediately that this was not going to resemble the journey where White Owl first came to me. I had a sense this was going to be very intense. There was no turning back now.

As I began to sink into the Earth, I felt the sensual waves of energy course through my body as the elementals began to dance me. The sounds that came out of my mouth were amazing. They laughed and cooed and sang through me. The sensations were pure pleasure.

Later, this shifted and I went into my pain, which was once again overwhelming and excruciating. The medicine took me deep into it. My body was racked with sobs and the next thing I knew, Amelia had slipped into my bed putting her arm around me and the other hand on my stomach. Compassion emanated from her as she began to work with me, and she knew just what to do.

I had a sense of myself as Persephone. I was in the depths of despair and Amelia felt like mother Demeter, holding her daughter and healing her with wisdom. I asked through my tears, "Amelia, when will Leif come back to me? Will he ever come back to me? How I miss him!"

"Honey, he can't meet you where you are. You just have to let him go and love him." That spun me deeper into despair. I didn't want to accept it.

I kept asking her the same questions. I would focus on the pain and then come out of it, then return to it again. Intermittently, I would come out and ask, "Where is he? Where is he?"

Amelia would answer, "You have to love him from where you are. Just be love. It's always his choice whether he's going to receive and open to it or remain where he is."

As I swam in my despair, she said, "Listen. The attachment is to the cord between the two of you, so let's release the cord. It's your choice how long you want to be attached to it."

"If I release the cord, will he come back?"

"He might, but you won't feel the same. You won't feel the pull of the cord, so you'll be able to greet him from a totally different place."

I was deep in the recesses of my psyche and the part of me asking the questions was the wounded little girl. Fortunately, I was talking to a compassionate, wise woman. As the waves of the medicine got more intense, we went into ourselves even deeper. I kept choosing to touch the pain, while Amelia kept telling me that the pain is an illusion.

She later explained that she was with me in the hallways of my deep psyche. She went in there to midwife me through this painful piece. This is not something just anyone can do. Amelia knew me well and knew she could trust me. She also knew herself enough to not identify with my personal material.

Another wave of pain came to me and Amelia had me breathe and expand myself. Responding to this, I shifted completely. My knees went up and I felt myself about to give birth.

I said to her, "You're birthing me," and she said, "No, Shonagh. You're birthing YOU."

I let the energy move through me and then I birthed it through and outward. In that moment, everything around me became luminous light. It was shimmering and beautiful. I felt like I had just given birth to a new version of myself.

After this, things shifted markedly. Amelia later said that it was at this point that she felt all the warm, beautiful, light places within me. She then sensed there was one area within me where I would need to go in order to bust through the place where I give my power away. She watched me go there and that's when everything changed.

I felt myself as an old woman in a hospital bed—dying. Amelia was still with me, speaking her wisdom. I began to think she was a death midwife. I told her so and she said, "Shonagh, you know how to move through this. This can go however you want. You have a choice here. We can bring in music, or light, whatever you want to assist you with this."

That answer had me convinced I was dying and I began to project the angel of death onto her. I got out of bed and turned on the light to see myself in the mirror. I didn't look old but I was certain I was experiencing myself as an aged, dying woman in a hospital.

This is something I actually dread experiencing in real life. My deep psyche brought it forward for me to move through.

At that moment I lost trust for her. I was deep in the medicine and deep in my place of projection now. I went to open the bedroom door and Amelia said, "Shonagh, I wouldn't go out there if I were you."

I proceeded to walk out of the safety and comfort of the bedroom and into the darkened hallway. Fortunately at the time, Richard was out for the evening so we had the house to ourselves.

Amelia said later that she knew I was about to bust through into another reality. She knew that on some level the part of me that was directing this had the courage and the wisdom to go there fully. She understood what she would have to do to protect me but also had the wisdom to know when to let me go and manage her own care before she came back to me. I proceeded to go through a series of "realities" that were desperately grim.

Walking down my hallway, I turned on the light. Everything looked decrepit. The energy felt heavy and depressing, like the place had been abandoned. I realized later I was picking up on the energy of my split with Richard, which permeated the house.

Amelia came to me and suggested I drink some water and eat something. She wanted to get me grounded. I had my arms folded across my chest and refused. I had a sense of myself as a teenage girl in a mental hospital and Amelia was trying to get me to take some medication. I thought maybe I had OD'd on something and was now institutionalized. I steadfastly refused water and food and proceeded to make my way to the kitchen.

I walked in and turned on the light. It looked horrible to me. I had always hated my brown granite counter and it looked just ghastly now. Amelia had followed me into the kitchen and was trying to coax me back into the bedroom. Seeing my kitchen as utterly decrepit, it occurred to me that I had invited a dark curse into my house. This put me into utter despair. I kept saying to myself, "What have I done? What have I done?" The part of me that didn't believe in myself was convinced I'd fucked up somehow and brought in a curse. I wondered if I had picked it up in Belize.

Amelia would not stop telling me to come back to the bedroom and that was when I began to think she was the demon of the curse that I had brought through. We walked into the front foyer, which was an expansive space with cathedral ceilings and skylights. Amelia began physically trying to pull me to the room. I would say, "All right. Okay," and then I would say, "No."

"Shonagh, you brought me here because you trusted me and you knew who to bring with you. I am NOT going to leave here." This convinced me that she was the demon of the curse and I was destined to spend eternity with her in this decrepit house with no daylight, only the black of night. Amelia was beginning to see my perception of her was markedly skewed.

She later told me that she saw the large foyer we were in as a hallway of expansion. With that realization she blew wide open and experienced universal consciousness. It came to her that we were together so we could "remember" each other. She knew how wise and powerful we were and that she was to let me go down the hallways of my deep psyche—she would simply hold my tether. She went back to the bedroom to do some self-care and when she ventured down the hall to check on me she realized, "Woo hoo! We're here! Shonagh is in DEEP."

By now I had walked into the darkened master bedroom where Richard slept alone. Fortunately, he still wasn't home. I looked around the room, which was messy and depressing. I felt the weight of unhappiness around my marriage and I almost fell to my knees on the floor. I walked over to the window seat to just sit in the feeling of that. It was a very heavy, sad energy. In my mind I visited all the anger and resentment we both projected onto each other. It was overwhelming to sit in those energies.

Looking out the window I remembered that Richard had recently hacked away all the shrubbery that grew around our large pond in the backyard. I discovered it when I got home from Belize and I'd cried when I saw what he'd done. Remembering that now, I opened the door to the back deck, stepping outside. I sat on the bench and mourned the loss of all the beautiful shrubs. I felt the nature spirits and tuned in to them. They did not feel pleased. There were no more hiding places for the ducks and other animals of the pond. No camouflage. No little nesting places. I made a promise to do a healing for them later.

My perception switched completely when I walked back into the bedroom. I felt myself as an older alcoholic woman who has abused alcohol to the point where she lives alone in a home that is falling apart. I thought that my girls were gone forever and my house would continue to deteriorate till I ended up on the street.

Amelia came in at one point and told me to drink some water. I saw her as the "spirit" of the alcohol tempting me to drink again. I had keyed deeply into the essence of addiction and was experiencing the devastation of the drinker as well as the energy of the spirits that tempted her.

Leaving the bedroom I made my way to the family room where I held my monthly full-moon ceremonies. I walked into that room and turned on the light. Richard's son, Jack, would hang out in that room watching TV and playing video games. It was a mess and I was disgusted. In that moment, Richard arrived home from his evening. He saw me and made his way through the back hall to say hello.

I saw him as **"the one who savaged the nature spirits by our pond"** and to my altered mind, he had brought in the darkness outside as well.

"Shonagh?"

I stared daggers at him and asked, "What have you done?" He had no clue what I was talking about and thought I was having a psychic break. At that moment, Amelia entered the room. She explained to Richard that I was on the medicine. He asked if I was going to be okay and she told him I would be fine.

She explained that she was also very altered but she knew she had to become lucid enough to meet him in his reality and get him to understand what was going on.

Amelia later said that she saw Richard's facial expression change to understanding and he went into neutrality. This was a great relief, for he was able to remain calm and composed. Richard later joked that he thought he'd come home to a David Lynch movie.

Meanwhile, in the depths of my psyche I had decided that the two of them were in cahoots and were now my dark keepers. I was back to the perception that I had brought in a dark curse. It was so real to me. Richard was calm and that plummeted me into more despair, as he felt cold and mocking. I looked at the dark outside the window and asked him again, "What have you done?"

Amelia guided me back to our room and Richard followed. He asked her if there was anything he could do and she said she'd handle it from there.

I locked eyes with Richard one more time, sending out my anger and hatred and said, thinking of the hack-job by the pond, "You've betrayed me." I was really livid about this and I felt there was a nature spirit inside me that was expressing through me. Fortunately, Richard stayed calm and left us to ourselves.

I lay on my bed in our brightly lit room while Amelia talked to me. By now she had chosen to be in the frequency of love. She did not want to be drawn into the dark frequency that I was carrying or we'd both be in trouble. She knew I was deep in my own darkness and she understood that I would find my way back to her through the love vibration.

"Shonagh, just be love. Remember that you're love. Don't judge any of this. Just be love."

I was still projecting onto her as "the demon of the curse," so her words sounded like she was mocking me. Every time she *would say something to remind me who I was, I took it as her mockery. It was awful, and I lay on my bed in a state of loss.*

Mercifully, the medicine began to wear off and I looked up to see Amelia sitting on her bed. I asked if I could sit beside her and she made room for me. We turned off the lamp and lit a candle and spent the next couple of hours discussing the journey.

To my surprise, Amelia said, "Shonagh, holy shit! What amazing work you did! You took me right with you and I cracked wide open tonight."

"Oh no, I'm so sorry you had to come with me!"

"No, Shonagh. I'm so grateful to you. You went right into your darkness and you totally let yourself go there. I am in awe of your bravery and courage to just go for it like that. It's so beautiful!"

I told her about what I'd experienced and that I'd thought she was part of a curse I'd brought in. Amelia laughed and told me how hard she tried to get me to come back to the room and shift but I was "one stubborn motherfucker." I laughed and said that was my Aries ram.

Then I remembered Richard and lamented that he'd seen us. I was sure I'd be in big trouble in the morning. Amelia in her wisdom said, "Shonagh, so what. You're getting divorced. You are afraid of his judgment, but this is your *own* judgment. Let it go. And who cares what he thinks. This was a *huge* piece for you tonight. You dove head first into your shadow. That took courage. You faced your own darkness. You rock!"

We finally went to bed and at one point Amelia got up to use the bathroom. In that moment I heard my cat mewing outside our window. I got up and walked to the front door to let her in. Then, with perfect timing, just as I opened the door, I heard an owl call. White Owl had been with me the whole time.

The following morning, with very little sleep, I awoke at six-thirty, thinking about Richard. Something in me had shifted and I realized I'd been viewing him through my wound for these past few years. Now I felt only compassion for him. I got out of bed and made my way to my office. I sat down at my computer and wrote him this letter:

Richard,

I want to tell you how sorry I am for all the devastation and pain of our marriage. I faced my deepest despair of that last night. I never should have left the comfort and beauty of my little room but I made myself walk through the house and felt into the loss all around me. Our bedroom was the hardest and I made myself sit at the window and fucking feel that. I left the door open, I am so sorry.

Our paths intersected last night to my horror and . . . it was no accident. There is a healing that needs to happen with us before we part ways. I wanted to knock on your door this morning and hug you and say how sorry I am . . . for everything, but I didn't think you'd appreciate it.

I opened myself to my deepest pain around our marriage last night and in so doing, I later felt yours. I keyed into my projection, my anger, my judgment, and my despair. So much anger at not being seen by you—I am sorry for that.

And so much of what I have felt over the years, you have felt as well . . .

This has brought me to my knees. The healing here is my apology to you. It is not important if you do not accept it. What is important is that I am sincerely sorry . . .

Love brings up everything unlike itself. Truly so. And I understand how this is serving us. We are expanding, Richard. Through great pain, I'm afraid . . . we are expanding, making room for more light to come in when our hearts break like this.

I don't question anymore why things happen the way they do. I trust Spirit, no matter how fucked up life feels at times. I sit here and I can say that I cracked open so wide last night that I only feel compassion for you, and compassion for myself. This is not easy, what we have chosen, and I mean all of it—the coming together, the marriage, the disagreements, the anger, the resentments. And then there has to be a reckoning and a light of understanding, and I received it, as scared and frightened as I was last night. I got it through that experience.

I am beginning to see how adversity gifts us. It attempts to crack us open and if it does truly crack us to our heart, we can see, we can experience that transcendent light of understanding. I hope I am making sense here.

Well, if your door wasn't locked, I would hug you. So I will hug you from my heart and thank you for this incredible, terrible time together. Wink. Wink. I am smiling here. I can actually smile through this pain of what has been created in order to bring us to the next level, the next place in our lives. It is not together in marriage, but we have weathered a great windy path together. It ain't over yet, but we're getting there. We're both working so hard to know ourselves, just in different ways.

I feel my vulnerability in sharing with you in this way because your judgment just kills me, it really does. And . . . mine is pretty crushing for you. How perfect we have been for each other, Richard—our wounds duking it out over and over.

My dear old friend, I am so very, very sorry.

After writing the note I walked back to the bedroom. Amelia woke up and I told her what I had written. She felt this was a major healing. We talked for a while and then I heard Richard's footsteps outside our door where the heat thermostat is.

"Richard? Would you like to come in here?"

"Yes, I would." He came in, sat on my bed, and to my astonishment, gave me a big hug. I cried more tears as he held me close. Then he pulled up a chair and the three of us talked for over three hours.

"I'll say this. I was NOT expecting that letter from you this morning," he said. "It was beautiful, thank you. After last night, I didn't know what I was going to wake up to today."

We laughed and talked about the medicine journey and its power to heal in such surprising ways. I then proceeded to tell Richard everything I had been experiencing over the last six months. I told him about my White Owl experience, my trip to Belize, and I told him about Leif.

Richard responded with compassion and understanding. He was very frank about the fact that he'd lost passion for the marriage, and he understood why I'd reached out to Leif. Amelia was witness to this beautiful unfolding and the three of us bonded that morning. It was a huge relief to have that transparency with Richard. I felt we'd turned a corner. I had wanted to end our marriage with consciousness and I was realizing that that is a process. We had to experience everything in order to get us to a place where we could end our marriage consciously. We were at that place now.

Richard asked if we could all have breakfast together and we made our way to the kitchen. For the first time in months, I was able to sit across from him and feel only friendship. We were buoyant and grateful for what had unfolded.

I drove Amelia home and when I got back I knew it was time to call Leif. I set my intention and gave him a call. He had received the email I'd sent and wanted to know what was up. I told him that I knew he didn't want me in his life anymore.

I told him I loved him very much and was sad to say good-bye. Leif asked if I'd be coming to see him at some point and I said, incredulously, "Leif, I won't be out there for a long time! I have to heal. My heart is broken. I've cried so many tears over you since that week in December, you have no idea."

He awkwardly apologized but I felt his irritation.

I kept the conversation as short as possible. I was crying and he was not responding with much warmth. He told me he loved me very much but he felt like he couldn't give me what I wanted. I told him I wanted to be his lover, to come visit him once a month and be a part of his life. I knew as soon as I said that, he wanted none of it. We finished the call saying we loved each other, and that was the end of the conversation. I would not call him again. It was time to move on.

Immediately upon hanging up, I called my friend, Melissa, in tears. I told her about the medicine journey and my phone call with Leif. Melissa is seventy-four years old. She is a very advanced spiritual seeker, having studied with teacher, Brugh Joy, for over twenty-five years. She possessed incredible wisdom combined with a gruff frankness that I cherished.

I told her through my tears about my conversation with Leif and she asked impatiently, "When are you going to stop crying over him?"

"Well, when the pain goes away," I stammered.

"Shonagh, you are attached to him. You have to cut the cord. You're draining him with this longing! He can feel it energetically."

She told me to set a date on the calendar for when I'm going to officially stop crying. I suggested the Spring Equinox but she said that was too soon and I'd be setting myself up for failure. My birthday was in two weeks and I decided to make that my date. Melissa thought that was perfect.

Then she told me I would need to take a break from the medicine for at least six weeks, as I was associating it with Leif. I had to make my own association with the medicine now. It was my medicine, my calling. I had to own that.

Melissa was so right and so wise. I was deeply grateful for her no-nonsense advice. I later called Amelia to make an appointment to dissolve the cords to Leif. This is something I do for my clients but could not do for myself. Amelia would be thorough in her approach. We would do it later that week. I felt sadness but the healing was already beginning to happen for me.

I thought of Amelia's words from the medicine journey and tuned into the frequency of love. I let myself be love. I thought of Leif and said, "I release you with blessings and love, Leif. Thank you."

That would be my mantra for as long as I needed. Love was the truth of who I was and it was the path I chose to walk. Everything that had come to me was from love. I knelt in front of my altar and asked White Owl for strength and guidance, and I thanked her for guiding me so powerfully.

⇒ 22 ⇐

Dissolving the Cords

*Your grief for what you've lost lifts a mirror up to where
you're bravely working.*
*Expecting the worst, you look, and instead here's the joyful
face you've been wanting to see.*
Your hand opens and closes and opens and closes.
*If it were always a fist or always stretched open, you'd be
paralyzed.*
*Your deepest presence is in every small contracting and
expanding, the two as beautifully balanced and coordinated
as bird wings.*

—Rumi

Before Amelia arrived to do the cord dissolving, I had to make a trip to the post office to pick up two packages Leif had sent me. I'd asked him to send me the kitchen knife and the ring. He sent me an email saying he had put two insured boxes in the mail and I would receive them the following day. This worried me greatly. I had requested two small things. I feared he had gathered all my gifts and had sent them all back.

When I got the boxes home I opened the first one and was crestfallen to see he'd sent back a Thangka of the

Tibetan goddess, White Tara, that I had given him. The second box sent me reeling. At the top was the beautiful medicine-gathering bag I'd given him for Christmas. That killed me. Also included was a Oaxacan carved frog I'd gifted him in the fall. He was visibly touched when he'd opened that present. I was stunned to see it returned.

My ring was there, thoughtfully taped to a beautiful snail shell. My knife was included, as were a few other gifts I'd given him. He'd also put in a few things I'd left at his house. I was knocked sideways by the contents. I had the sensation of someone punching me in the stomach as hard as they could.

He had included a letter saying how much he loved me and that he'd never intended to hurt me. He said that he didn't feel right keeping all of the beautiful medicine pieces I'd gifted him. He wanted me to know he was honored and grateful and meant no disrespect in returning them.

Without hesitation, I called him in tears. The conversation was fraught with emotion as I struggled to understand. He explained that he loved me very much. He had no intention of ending our relationship but he was going through a lot internally and needed his space. He said it hurt him when he saw my email requesting the gold ring back. He figured I'd want some of the other gifts back as well. It was clear from the conversation that our lack of communication was fueling assumptions on both sides. What a mess.

He asked me to please be patient and give him some time. He wanted me to come visit in April but I was too upset to make that plan. He was very clear that he was going through a difficult time right now and couldn't give me what I wanted. He felt I was trying to change him, which I denied vehemently. We talked for a while longer and ended the conversation as calmly as possible.

When Amelia arrived, I let her know what had happened. What perfect timing for this ritual. I was as ready as I was ever going to be to release these dysfunctional cords of connection to Leif. It was my hope that I could greet him from a different place, one of empowerment rather than grasping.

The energetic connection between two people is called "cording." The love we feel for another forms a cord connecting both hearts. Thoughts we have about our lover or friend can turn into cords, particularly if we ponder that thought often or obsess about them in some way. Thoughts are powerful and they manifest not only situations and events, but also energy that forms a cord that attaches into another.

This connection is why people often know when their lover or friend has passed away. One just "knows" their lover is cheating or ill or in trouble because of the cords that connect them. When people cord to each other, they often form attachments. Not all of our cords are connected from a place of integrity. We sometimes manipulate each other. When we become aware of our dysfunctional cording, we can dissolve that cord and correct the behavior.

One of the best books I've seen that illustrates these cords is artist, Alex Grey's book, *Transfigurations*. Throughout the book there are extraordinary depictions of people with radiant light all around them. There is an exquisite picture of a woman giving birth, and the cords connecting mother and child are clearly shown. Energy is a powerful, beautiful thing. Just because it can't be seen with human eyes doesn't mean it isn't present. The more

we understand it, the more enhanced our life become ~~cords~~ ~~trans~~ ~~mute~~ ~~energy~~
we learn to work with it to create balance and harmony.

For my situation with Leif, the actual cord of love between us would be left alone. It was the secondary cords that I knew stemmed from the places in me that needed healing. Those cords needed to be dissolved now. Amelia was a master adept with this work and I was grateful to have her expertise.

Most people who practice energy medicine talk about *cutting* cords. In the technique that Amelia used, the cords were *dissolved,* and there is a reason for this. Her teacher, Anaiis Salles, who designed this process, wisely noted that the act of "cutting" is a violent act. You are cutting something and that sends out shock waves. The energetic cords can fly outward, entangling with other cords.

With the process of dissolving, it is gentle but thorough. The work is accompanied by an awareness of where our cords to our lover originated within ourselves. This tells us much about our own misuse of our power. There is no judgment; it's not about judging. It's about becoming self-aware, seeing where we need to make a correction, and then transmuting the energy.

Rather than do it for me, Amelia had me dissolve the cords, which was very empowering. She simply guided me through it. She worked with instructions from another fabulous teacher, Joy Caffrey, who has the cord-dissolving process on her website, www.JoyfulHealingCenter.com. We began with me lying on the table and grounding myself into the Earth. Then I brought my attention into my heart center, calling on the wisdom and grace of the heart to guide me through this.

Amelia instructed me to call in the image of Leif, bringing him about ten feet from me, where I could look into his eyes. This brought my sadness to the surface and I was told not to judge it, but to simply let it pass through me. Then Amelia told me to scan my body for any areas of discomfort. When I had located a specific area, she had me put an etheric hand of light into that place and unhook the cord that belonged to Leif, dissolving it back to him.

I did this a couple of times and with each cord I dissolved, I was instructed to look into Leif's eyes and repeat a series of declarations that empowered the process. I then lit a fuse at the end of the cord and let it burn/transmute its way back to Leif.

Then we reversed the process, and it was this piece that offered me the self-awareness I required. Scanning Leif's energy body now, I felt for places in him where I had connected my cords. Once located, I reached my etheric hand to where they had attached. I released the cord and lit the fuse, letting the cord burn back to me. I had to feel into myself to where each cord originated. The first one originated in my second chakra, which is the area of creativity and sexual power. I understood immediately that this cord was about manipulating with my sexual energy.

Another cord I brought back originated in my third chakra, which is personal power. There was some misuse of my power with Leif here as well. I began crying tears of shame, but Amelia told me, "Shonagh, this is not about judging yourself. We all do this."

When it was complete, I set an intention to connect to Leif with unconditional love, empowerment, and compassion. I held the intention in my heart and sent it to his heart with a cord of light.

When the process was complete, I felt totally different. The anxiety I felt around him was gone. I could see with clarity how the various unhealed aspects within myself cord into another, using manipulation to get what I need. Around that realization was self-love. I held no judgment of myself about any of this. It was the suchness of where I was at the time and I was in a place now where I could heal.

The rest of the day, I felt a lightness of being. My anxiety and soul-pain over Leif was gone. Gone. My addled brain was clearing up, and for the first time since I'd last seen him, I didn't long for him. That night I lay in bed and spoke to Mother Earth and White Owl. I thanked them for the gift of Amelia and what she had done for me that day. Then I asked them to tell me about Leif's role in my life. I fell into a deep sleep and awakened in the wee hours with a beautiful dream.

Leif has brought me to his mother, who is reclined on a chaise, wearing a long white dress. I go and sit by her. She leans into me and kisses me on the lips. Then I hold her hands and kiss her fingers. Leif stands by, regarding us lovingly.

In the dream, Leif's mother is not his literal mother. I understood immediately the dream was saying that Leif brought me to direct engagement with the Divine Mother. She was my "sweet mama" who spoke to me on the medicine and engaged my kundalini in a tantric experience of ecstatic bliss. She was the Earth Mother whom I looked to each night to fill me.

Growing up, I had always been close to Mother Mary. I was unmoved by everything the Catholic Church had to offer except her. Looking back, I understand that part of my consciousness recognized Mary as Mother Goddess. For the past ten years I have engaged the goddess, whom I think of as Divine Mother. I have a profound connection with the Mayan mother goddess, Ix Chel, who is mother of the Earth and moon. I worship Her as Mother Earth and think of myself as Her daughter. Leif brought me to the medicine, which opened me powerfully to *direct engagement* with Her. I have never felt so close to Her as I have since I began working with the sacred mushrooms.

White Owl comes to me as my sister and she too feels like a goddess. The mystery is still unfolding for me but I know that because of Leif, I have been irrevocably shifted. I woke the next day with what I can only describe as a larger love for him. I felt humbled by the mystery of who we were. I knew that Leif and I were meant to come together and awaken each other in very profound ways. With that realization, I felt no anger or upset around him. I only felt gratitude and appreciation for what he had brought me to.

These last three months, where I felt myself in an underworld of personal pain—a classic, dark night of the soul—had served to bring me to an unprecedented opening of my awareness. Through my emotional journey with Leif, and my profound journeys on the medicine, I was being guided more deeply into the mystery of Self and my connection to the Sacred. My intuitive capacities were expanding greatly and I was learning to self-nurture by calling in Spirit to soothe me when I was in need. This was an essential piece for me to master.

That morning it all came in and I was overwhelmed by the divine dance of life. I thought back to the previous summer, when I began doing the medicine with Leif, and smiled at the perfect choreography of events up to this point. I sensed that everything was in divine order. I knew that whatever happened between us beyond that moment, we would always think of each other with great love and gratitude.

I was free of the cords of my own dysfunction. I could now greet Leif from an empowered place where I knew myself as a beloved daughter of the Divine Mother. Leif had given me this gift. I felt truly whole for the first time ever.

⤳ 23 ⤳

Shifting Energies

Fostering the creative imagination, therefore, becomes an exciting and potentially revolutionary act. But, as with all creative acts, it depends on death as well as birth: the conscious surrender and dissolution of old concepts and patterns of thinking and doing, so that new ones, more in tune with the deepest interests, the I AM of the people, may have space to be seen and heard. To imagine new forms of parenting and human relating, for example, requires letting go of old ones, risking the shifting ground as well as containing the emptiness, the waiting receptivity, so as to create a womb in which the new may be conceived and gestate.
—Sukie Colegrave, *By Way of Pain: A Passage into Self*

After the cord-dissolving session with Amelia, everything shifted. My relationship with Leif as I knew it was over. If we chose to return to each other, it would be from a new place. I could look back on what had happened and see that the entire experience carried immense teachings.

I decided to send a box of items to Leif along with a letter, telling him about the cord dissolving. In the letter I admitted I'd been trying to change him, hoping he would be the same person he'd been in the fall. I told him he wasn't responsible for my happiness but I had made him so and I apologized for that. I told him I loved him no matter what he chose to do.

In the box I put the medicine-gathering bag and the Oaxacan frog. I added some Amish butter that he loved, as well as a conch shell. In Belize Leif had seen conch shells all over the island of Caye Calker and wanted to bring one home. He never did, so I gifted him a beautiful shell I'd kept for many years. It would be a symbol of slow and steady movement forward, in whatever form our relationship was to take.

The box arrived three days later and Leif called me, saying that he had felt the cords go the previous week. He'd experienced a sudden clarity and strength and wondered at the time if maybe I'd cut the cords. We talked for over an hour with the ease of two good friends. I felt love for him but no yearning, no anxiety, and no neediness. When I hung up I felt clear and grounded.

That night, my phone rang. By now I was so accustomed to rarely talking with Leif that it didn't occur to me he would be calling. I was pleasantly surprised to hear his voice twice in one day. He was in good cheer and simply wanted to tell me how much he loved me. He must have told me twenty times during the conversation. He asked me when I could come out in April, saying he was looking forward to some "Shonagh skin." Leif assured me we were good and talked about building me a chicken coop when I moved to my next place. He seemed intent on assuring me of his love. We spoke for over an hour and again I noticed how shifted we both were.

This was big for me. I knew just how easy it was to bond with another and then go unconscious as each person's wounds were triggered. Leif and I had been given the opportunity to initiate healing in each other. It was a hell of a process but I could feel that I'd come through it a lot more conscious than I was before.

By now I was in the habit of looking to Spirit to fill me. I'd had a realization about the void I felt within—that void was for Spirit. There was no one on this Earth who could fill it, nor would any one thing fill it either. On a daily basis I was surrendering to Spirit, calling in White Owl for guidance and wisdom. My nightly ritual of infusing myself with the Earth's love was very nourishing. I was giving myself the care and love that no one else was equipped to give me. In doing so, I could see Leif more clearly now and love him from a healthier place.

I began to express a joy and a humor that people noticed immediately. I taught a medicine-wheel weekend and my students commented on how happy I was. Interestingly, the direction for that weekend was the north. In the Peruvian medicine-wheel training, the north is about claiming your place in your lineage of ancestors and answering your calling. It is about gathering and cultivating personal power and not colluding with the collective. The archetype for the north is the hummingbird, which takes the epic journey, and does so with joy. This is about taking ownership of who we are as a quantum being and connecting to the joy that lives in each of us.

Over the course of the weekend I gave the women exercises to bring them more deeply into their power. The frequency of joy colored the whole weekend and they were ebullient. They experienced profound shifts within as they engaged sacred rituals and healing practices. The joy emanating from each woman was contagious. I felt myself deepening into my own power through the process. I felt as if Spirit had handed me the most exquisite magic wand, saying, "Hey, you left this behind when you incarnated. I've been trying to get your attention, but you're a tough nut to crack. Well, here it is, beautiful. Use it wisely."

The following day I experienced a dramatic shift that I never would have expected. My stepdaughter, Claire, had emailed me a week earlier to say she wanted to meet and make an amends. This was not to be underestimated for either of us. The years I'd struggled with her and her father had been the worst years of my life. My marriage to Richard was as good as over by the time she'd moved out.

After my medicine-wheel students left, I had done my own cord dissolving for my relationship with Claire in preparation for our meeting on Monday morning. I wanted to clear any energetic cords of dysfunction so I could greet her from the clearest place possible. And I wanted to send a cord of light to her that held the energy of unconditional love, compassion, and empowerment. That part of the cord work was deeply meaningful to me because I knew its power to shift the dynamic was very real.

I felt the healing from our amends would span lifetimes. A few years ago, when I was in the thick of the trouble with her, I had taken a class for shamanic journeying. The teacher guided us on a journey to the Akashic Library. This is the place in the ethers where every record of every lifetime we've ever lived is kept. I saw myself there and I was looking through a large book of my lifetimes when the name "Claire" came into my awareness. I thought to myself, "Goddamnit, not *here*! Can't I get some respite from her?"

Instantly I saw myself as a man in another life. I was walking away from the scene of Claire's death. She too was a man in that life and I'd just had her killed. I saw that we were sworn enemies. She had anticipated her own killing and had arranged for mine. As I was walking away from the scene of her death, six men ambushed me. I took an uppercut from an axe that struck me under the front of my neck and cut my head clear off my body. Then I saw the words, "NO RESOLUTION." I was horrified, and I remember saying to Spirit, "So you put us together in the same *family?*"

A month after that experience I had an astrology/ intuitive reading with my friend, Sydney. I had emailed her about an incident that had occurred with Claire, which had resulted in a hell of a fight between Richard and me. I remember writing in the subject line of my email to her, "Crisis."

Sydney wrote me a reassuring letter back, saying, "Shonagh, do you see the *Isis* in 'crisis'?" She loved to play with words and she was pointing out the gift in every challenge we face.

When she did my reading, she had both our charts together. She said that whenever she sees that level of hatred between two charts, she knows that the first lifetime was one of deep love. Then a betrayal happened, and every lifetime following, it was always the betrayal that was remembered and never the love. She said we had a myriad of lifetimes with intense hatred and competition— often to the death.

Sydney told me that this was the lifetime where we would be able to heal this rift for good. I found that hard to believe, given the circumstances. She laughed and said that Claire was "the greatest homeopathic remedy of this lifetime" for me. Any time Claire pushed one of my buttons, I was told to leave the room and find a private place. I was to think of my chest as a type of control panel where all my buttons were kept. Then I was to pull out the button she'd just pushed. I was to ask the goddess, "What is *this* about?" Sydney told me to wait and I'd receive an answer.

Once I had the answer, I had a choice. I could choose to put the button back, but it would be much harder to take out next time. Or I could choose to burn it in the etheric fires, or give it to Mother Earth to mulch and make flowers with. Sydney said if I did that every time a button was pushed, eventually I would have none left. A shaman had taught that to her and she passed it on to me. I had found this to be very helpful the few times I used it. Most of the time, however, I was so caught up in the drama of the triangulation of the three of us, I'd spiral into my perceived powerlessness.

The time had finally come where both Claire and I had done enough of our own self-healing that we could greet each other from a place of forgiveness and compassion. She arrived promptly at ten with an air of humility and softness to her. I was struck by the transformation from rage-filled teenager to gentle young woman whose sincerity was very evident. I admired her courage for coming to me in this way. This was no small act for either of us. I invited her into my office and, bless her heart, she had a notebook where she had written everything she wanted to say to me. She clearly didn't want to forget anything. I was very touched and I felt my tears welling as I watched hers fall.

She proceeded to apologize for a number of things, her admission of such a testament to the impressive inner growth she had cultivated. I then apologized to her, wishing I had done a better job of handling the events over those years. I told her she looked like a butterfly that had emerged from the chrysalis. I said that she looked utterly transformed and I was very impressed with everything she'd done to get herself to that place. I meant every word, feeling only love and compassion for her.

We talked about how pain serves us, and I told her the story of Rumi and Shams. She had never heard of Rumi, so I gifted her with a book of his poems. Then Claire asked me what I'd been up to. She seemed genuinely interested. I spoke for a bit and then asked her the same question. Our conversation was easy and sincere. We sat there, both of us feeling the relief of letting this burden go once and for all.

The amends had gone beautifully. We gave each other a hug and I held her to me, sending love from my heart to hers. I cannot adequately describe how good it felt to hold Claire in my arms like that. The healing went very deep.

A couple of days later I was to leave for a visit to see Leif. I actually had some trepidation about it and I drew a couple of Tarot cards, asking how it would go. The cards did not offer any encouragement. Leif ended up sick with a horrible cough and sleepless nights and I was going to postpone coming. Later that day, we spoke, and he sounded much worse. He was at the point of needing someone to care for him. We agreed that I would come that night with all my good medicines.

I was there for just a couple of days and as the cards had indicated, it ended badly. I'd felt an all-too-familiar loneliness creeping in that last night with Leif. I felt he was doing a push-pull with me, which was emotionally wrenching. The following morning I again felt he had no romantic interest in me. We met each other with distance as our wounds opened once again.

When I began a discussion with him I was met with callous words of anger. This triggered my defenses and the morning fell apart. I left his home stinging from his remarks, but I was not in the abyss I'd entered when I'd left his home in January. I could feel a foundation within myself. I also had a realization that what is created energetically manifests slightly later in the physical. The work I'd done interiorly was shifting things and would take a bit more time to cement in the 3D.

Driving away from his home, I had a feeling this experience was exactly what I needed to finally release him. Rather than beat myself up for being foolish, I decided to acknowledge the grace of this.

I arrived home feeling sad but also clear. Creating my new life was to be my focus and all my energy was to be directed to that end. It was that simple. I felt complete with this and I knew I had made an important internal shift. All the work I had done over the last three months was enabling me to finally let him go. The cord dissolving had made this last experience much easier to handle.

I thought of something one of my teachers recently said to me. I'd reached out to him about a different situation where I'd given my power away momentarily to someone with a superiority complex. This man wielded his arrogance and judgment of me with all the righteousness he could muster. My teacher said, "Shonagh, you have forgotten who you are in the face of judgment. Don't you remember your Mayan baptism at the sacred caves at Uxmal? Don't you remember the blessings I have given you? Do you remember the blessing from Don Florencio? I have given you these teachings, not to give you my power, but to open you to your own."

This piece with Leif was about coming into my own power. No wing-man necessary. I didn't need to be with him to do the medicine. I didn't need him in my life to feel strong and supported. I needed only to call up my own power—a balanced feminine/masculine power rich with its own wisdom and strength. Leif had been the gateway out of my marriage and into a whole new life, but it was apparent that he was not meant to walk any further down the path with me as my lover. I would always love him for what he had opened me to.

In the meantime, I was on a journey of consciousness expansion and this was of utmost importance to me. With the plant medicine I had unlocked great doorways within myself and I had only just scratched the surface. I had another medicine journey planned and I could feel that it was going to be different. The journey this time would not be to my pain.

I made an empowered decision to choose *consciousness* instead of lamenting a doomed relationship. Since beginning the medicine, I had changed much interiorly. Rather than numb myself with what society offers people in pain—liquor, antidepressants, shopping, and entertainment—I chose expansion of my awareness through plant medicine.

I thought about the culture in which I was raised. There was nothing in that culture that came remotely close to imbuing me with real meaning. It was a vapid, sterile culture obsessed with a pathetic media, with deplorable leadership on every level. As Terence McKenna once said, "We are led by the least among us."

I knew that if entheogens were readily available to people in Western culture, with an understanding and a respect for their healing powers, we would have a civilization of conscious people. Entheogens are mec cines of the heart. I have heard story after story of peop who engaged these medicines who were able to shift their inner workings and heal relationships. I realized that I carried my own story of how applicable this medicine is for shifting from destructive patterns of behavior and opening to a profound relationship with Self and Spirit.

In terms of my relationship to Spirit, I am in a place of total trust. I'm experiencing constant synchronicities and I can see Spirit assisting and guiding me at every turn. I regard every person as a teacher and every event in my life as a teaching. The medicine has deepened my relationship to Spirit more profoundly than any guru, priest, or teacher, because my engagement has been *direct* and it is *my own*. It is not based on anything that someone else is trying to convey. It is unique to me and it is sacred and holy.

I realize, as well, that everything I express in this life is sacred and holy. I am composed of both light and dark and both serve. If I commit a wrong, I can correct it without beating myself up. I see myself as a truly precious being, along with every living organism on this green Earth. As William Blake said in *The Marriage of Heaven and Hell*, "Everything that lives is holy." I am very much aware of my connection to the universe and every living being. This is the *unio mystica* and I have a window into it now.

That evening I knelt in front of my altar, and for the second time that day I dedicated myself to walking the beauty walk and living the beauty way. I surrendered myself once again to my beloved White Owl guide. I let myself feel waves of her love course through my body. I bid her to fill the void within me, after which I sank into a deep and restful night's sleep.

≈ 24 ≈

Nature Spirits and the Dragon

Shamanic ecstasy is the real "Old-Time Religion" of which modern churches are but pallid evocations. Shamanic visionary ecstasy, the mysterium tremendum, the unio mystica, the eternally delightful experience of the universe as energy, is a sine qua non of religion; it is what religion is for! There is no need for faith, it is the ecstatic experience itself that gives one faith in the intrinsic unity and integrity of the universe, in ourselves as integral parts of the whole; that reveals to us the sublime majesty of our universe, and the fluctuant, scintillant, alchemical miracle that is quotidian consciousness.

—Jonathan Ott, *The Age of Entheogens & The Angel's Dictionary*

I planned to do a medicine journey outside on my property with my good friend, Gina. I gave her a heads-up that I would be in a high shamanic trance state and that spirits might be coming through me. I wanted to make sure she knew I would be completely safe. I didn't want her to worry if I went deep into trance. I had a large pond in my back yard with an island in the center and a bridge that led to it. Gina and I set up a two-person tent on the island. We would be surrounded by water, which was home to countless frogs that would serenade us the entire night. I hoped the croaking would take me deep into the frog realms, as I held great affection for those creatures.

I had a good feeling about this journey. I was ready to go deep into Mother Earth and receive her medicine and I wanted to commune with the Earth spirits. It came to me to do six grams this time and I trusted the message and went ahead with it. We did a lovely ceremony, each of us calling in the spirits and speaking our intentions for the journey. I lit the copal to cleanse our fields. I blessed the mushrooms and called in protection for the space. Gina took a light dose and went into her journey fairly quickly.

I seemed to percolate for maybe forty-five minutes and then saw/felt a luminous white light over my head that came in for a split second and then disappeared. The frogs started croaking like crazy and I began to feel the fairies come into me.

The sounds coming out of my mouth were otherworldly and my entire body was in tantric bliss. The fairies danced me with abandon. I was writhing and cooing with their playful, sensual energy. At the same time, I was able to understand the songs of the frogs as they sang to each other from all around the pond. I could see an energetic arc of images from their songs that went from one side of the pond to the other. I saw fish and insects and water in this arc. I was struck by how sexual the frogs were. They were very fun and joyful and I could feel the energy of spring and rebirth all around us. It was a sensual, earthy, nature energy that reveled in pleasure.

When the frogs went quiet, the fairies receded as well. I fell into an awareness of my relationship with Leif. I began to cry, but I was not in my wound. I felt him released from me as my lover, understanding that what he needed more than anything right now was a friend. I answered that I would be his friend forever. I felt Spirit "feeling" me and then She said, "Good. That has passed. You are good with it."

After this, I found myself deep inside Mother Earth. She spoke to me, saying, "I have a man for you. He will find you and he will reflect the beauty and majesty of your being. He will see into your heart as I do." I began to cry and thanked her, saying over and over how much I loved her. I was told that all I had to do was "shine" and he would find me.

The frogs resumed their croaking and with that the fairies returned, dancing me with exquisitely pleasurable tantric waves of ecstasy. My body was moving with the energetic waves coursing through me when I felt Gina throw a blanket over me. She asked if I was all right and I told her through the waves of pleasure, "Yes, I'm good. It's fairies and other spirits. They're all good, not to worry."

I kicked off the blanket and let myself be swept up in the bliss of these extraordinary energies. The fairies said to me with great mirth, "People are so unaware! If they knew of us, they would drop everything and play in our vibration."

Again the frogs went quiet and the fairies receded. It was then that I went into an awareness of lifetime after lifetime of indescribable agony and suffering under the Church. I was taken through what I was told were five centuries of lifetimes where darkness reigned under the lords of black magic who ran the Church. These were lives where I had been burned alive, thrown in jail in manacles, thrown in a ditch to die, torn apart, and tortured mercilessly.

I continued to move through many lifetimes where I had experienced horrific trauma. During all of it I had my legs open and realized I was birthing/releasing the stories. At one point I said out loud, "I have no more chains! The shackles are gone!" It was utterly bizarre to be so deep in the experience of that.

I could feel the incredible pain of manacles and other devices, along with the psychic agony, fear, and despair.

The frogs began to sing again and I got that they were assisting in the releasing of all of that. At one point I sat up and felt my throat and said, "The noose is gone!" My throat felt completely different. It was clear like I have never felt before, and I said, "They hung me!" I had been betrayed and it came to me that I had to forgive those people for what they'd done. I let go of that lifetime and sent forgiveness to my accusers and the executioner. I lay on my back feeling myself psychically unburdened from what seemed to be heavy geometries in my field.

Gina gave me words of encouragement and I began receiving memories of the two of us in numerous lifetimes where we had known each other. I felt in that moment how much we had been through together and my gratitude for her friendship and wisdom filled my heart.

Again the frogs sang their incredible songs and the fairies came into me again. I had not experienced this much fairy energy on the medicine and I delighted in it. I exclaimed to them as they came in, "I knew you were here!! I felt you but you were hiding!"

They were very playful and they filled every cell in my body with ecstasy and joy. I said to Gina, "Honey, the fairies LOVE you! You take such good care of the flowers and bees and they love you for that. I think that's why they're coming in so powerfully tonight. Isn't this so cool? Don't they sound amazing?"

The frogs went silent again and I sat up to listen. Gina started talking but I said, "Shhh, wait, sweetie. I'm listening to the frogs. They're telling secrets and I want to hear." It was then that I heard frogs singing in a neighboring pond. The frogs in my pond were hanging on to every croak. The neighbor frogs were singing to each other the songs of spring. Their energy was playful and almost teasing. The frogs in my pond answered with a raucous chorus of croaks. It was magnificent.

I fell back on my sleeping bag and went deep into trance. White Owl came to me and engaged me in conversation, giving me knowledge of my place in the cosmos. She also spoke of the karmic agreement between Leif and myself. In that moment I understood everything with perfect clarity. I cried for the suffering Leif had experienced in this life and I felt him as my brother. I would love him forever.

As I moved out of that awareness a most extraordinary thing happened. I had my hands on my belly and I said, "I can own my gift. I have a gift and I can own it and I won't be punished; in fact I will be rewarded."

As soon as I said this I felt myself birth a magnificent being. It was a sapphire blue, winged dragon with golden yellow eyes. It was the colors of the sapphire rings I wore. It felt female and I was awestruck by its size and beauty. She said, "I am no fantasy. You will ride me with humility and grace, and dignity and kindness."

I was stunned. I responded, saying, "Dear goddess, I have a dragon! She is absolutely beautiful!"

Then I began to cry to Spirit, saying, "I'm not sure I can do this. Are you sure I can carry this gift?"

Spirit responded with kindness, saying, "It is done." I looked into the great dragon's eyes and then felt myself mount her, her great wings spreading far outward on either side of me. I was in a state of reverential awe. She told me she was as fierce as she was kind. She was ancient and she knew me well, explaining that in spite of what "costume" we come in wearing, it is our frequency signature that can be read by these beings.

She told me that all around the planet, dragons are being birthed. They live within the Earth and they are coming out now. She said there are some very fierce dragons out there that want their blood back. Their blood is the oil and gas and they have had enough. I was told that we were in for a wild ride in terms of Earth changes. I felt fine with it. I had no fear of death after this many medicine journeys. I also had the knowing that I would be around for a good while longer.

The dragon told me we were in the birthing stage of a new era, saying that the old guard must go. I felt the sensation of an unimaginably vast force all around me and then heard the words, "She has become." I understood that to mean that the forces of the feminine were rising and all the "New World Order" talk would not be enough to hold her at bay. With her would come a return to the old ways of honoring the Earth. I did not feel this was in any way a slight to the masculine forces. In fact, I felt a welcoming as the scales that were so grossly unbalanced sought equilibrium.

Then Mother Earth spoke to me again explaining the number six. I had been told to do six grams of the medicine and when I received her information I smiled in delight, exclaiming, "I knew it!! I must trust myself more, I was bang on!" Six was the Lovers card in the Tarot. It was a number of balance and harmony, the union of the sacred masculine with the sacred feminine. It was also the hexagram, which was the shape of the honeycomb my beloved bees constructed in their hives. It also represented the six-petalled lotus of the heart chakra. From now on I was to work with six grams or more and it would take me deep into the realms of spirit and knowing. This was where I would find my wise dragon. As this was said, the dragon declared once again with authority, "I am no fantasy." Her eyes penetrated mine and I knew it to be true.

I felt absolutely ebullient after all of this. I could not wipe the smile from my face. I said to Gina, "Sweetie, I am fine as frog-hair in this moment! I am happier than I have ever been!"

I was still in the medicine, but I asked for her phone so I could call Leif.

"Are you sure? You told me not to let you call him."

"That was if I was in tears wanting him to come back to me. I want to tell him I'll be his friend forever," I responded.

Gina dialed the number for me and I got his answering machine. I left a message saying I loved him and I would be his friend forever—that I understood that at this point what he needed most was a friend. I told him I birthed a dragon and that I was sitting on my island surrounded by croaking frogs. In that moment they fired up their chorus and I said, "Leif, listen to them! They're saying hello!" I held the phone up to the sound and then said, "You can call me any time, Leif. I love you."

Gina and I talked for another hour or more before we finally fell asleep. The following day I began working with the journey to bring its gifts into my reality. To a traditional shaman, the experiences would be thought of as alternative realities, the beings—the occupants of those realities. To the deep psyche, there is no difference between what is real and what is imagined. This is why ritual is so powerful. The deep psyche is aware of the elevated intention of ritual and responds accordingly.

In this journey I shed what felt like cellular imprinting of numerous past-life traumas. At one point, my throat became more palpably clear and open than I'd ever felt before. My deep psyche was responding to the experience and my whole being had the sensation of having shed a great weight.

The dragon is a hugely symbolic creature. It is found in every ancient culture, from the Mayans to the Norse. I was profoundly moved by the presence of the dragon that made itself known to me in the journey. Dragons signify power and potent magic. They are symbols of mastery and can be arbiters of transcendence from one level to another. This dragon made it very clear that I was to "ride" her with humility and grace and dignity and kindness. I took this to mean that I was coming into a high level of personal power and there was no room for arrogance or ego inflation. The journey left me much to ponder and once again I felt waves of gratitude for finding my way to the sacred mushrooms.

I spoke with Leif the following day and we talked for almost two hours. I had the opportunity now to relate to him without the projections and the accompanying stories that ensue. I was good with all of it. I knew my path moving forward was to continue my personal medicine explorations, endeavoring to integrate and learn from them. I was beginning to bring the experiences into my teaching and discovered I had much to cull from. I delighted in the unorthodox direction my life was taking. I had no interest in leading a "normal" life, whatever that is. That was a good thing, as my explorations over the course of the next few months would lead me to very strange territory indeed.

≈ 25 ≈

Eagle Clan Sister

We are the winged ones of heaven, your reflections in per-
fect love, the missing dimension needed for your wholeness.
We are the spiritual guardians of the earth. Welcome us
into your consciousness. Blend with us. Remember. Know
yourself as fully, truly human.
Awaken, humankind. The teachers of love circle round the
morning star. Spiraling down. Coming to rest. They land.
At the edge of your history's shore.
Fluttering into consciousness. The Bird Tribes return.

—Ken Carey, *Return of the Bird Tribes*

I planned to do another medicine journey on a Saturday
in May, the day before a solar eclipse. The timing felt
right and I invited my friends Sasha and Amelia to join
me. We would do the medicine in a tent on my island, as
that location was pure magic.

Sasha was curious about the medicine and wanted to
experience a light dose. She was very excited to spend an
enchanted night with Amelia and me and eager to hear
the fairies come through me. Sasha was a close friend,
and her daughters, Carly and Anna, were friends with my
older daughter, Maddie. She lived in a little farmhouse

and I would often find her at work in her garden, her dog and cat wrestling playfully nearby. She was a regular at my monthly full-moon ceremonies and a participant in my second medicine-wheel group. Sasha liked to say that she prayed for a cool neighbor and then I showed up. One of the many cool things about *her* was the fact that she was a fantastic drummer and a gifted poet.

Sasha would come to me for healing work every so often and it was always a deep experience for both of us. She had an older brother, Seth, who was in the process of drinking himself to death. He lived in an apartment over his parents' garage and could no longer take care of his teenage daughter, who lived in another state with her mother. Sasha had wanted me to do healing work on him, but it never panned out. I had the feeling he wanted to die. I felt that no amount of healing work was going to change the outcome. This was his path and only his soul knew the reasons why.

Sasha had a beautiful girlfriend named Alexis whom she loved very much. Their relationship was complicated, as Sasha still shared a house with her ex-girlfriend, while Alexis lived in Oregon. Alexis was concerned about Sasha trying the medicine with me. When Sasha finally chose to do so, Alexis got upset and stopped talking to her a few days before our journey. It didn't help that Alexis knew about the full-body orgasms I would experience on the mushrooms. That made her insecure, along with the idea that Sasha might somehow lose her mind as a result. Psychedelics have quite a stigma in our culture and most people regard them with suspicion and fear. Interestingly, the word, *psychedelic* means to make the mind clear or visible. *Psyche* is the Greek word for mind and *delos* means clear or visible. Unfortunately, the word *psychedelic* has

decidedly pejorative connotations to most people—
including Alexis.

I had a sense that Amelia was not going to join us that
night and sure enough, she called that evening to say she
wasn't feeling up to it. I was not disappointed, as I always
trust Spirit and I knew in that moment that this evening
was between Sasha and me. When she arrived she told
me she had decided not to do the mushrooms. Instead,
she brought a cannabis cookie, figuring she'd eat that and
then hang out to see what came through me. I trusted her
judgment. Sasha was wise and she knew what she could
and could not handle.

We set up our sleeping bags in the tent and did a ceremony before doing the medicine. We smudged each other
and I used my white owl fan to walk the edges of the circular island to seal and protect our space with sage. We each
held our respective medicine and spoke our intentions for
the evening. I then hung my white owl fan from the ceiling of the tent. We consumed the medicines and lay down
to wait for the magic to begin.

Nothing happened for me and I waited for over an
hour. I began to wonder if maybe the strain of mushrooms
I had was weak. I began to feel badly, as I had shared with
Sasha how wonderful it was to hear the fairy beings and
other nature spirits that came through me.

She asked me a couple of times if anything was happening and I replied, "This is so strange. I've taken a huge
dose and there isn't a damn thing happening. No fairies! I
wonder if it's because I forgot to water the garden! Maybe
they're not happy with me."

*At some point I rolled over and dozed off. When I came
to, I felt myself in a room with the spirits. They were discussing
Sasha's prayers. Her prayers were always for her daughters,*

her brother, Seth, her parents, and her lovely, Alexis. I asked the spirits to please bless the people Sasha loved and shower my dear friend with their blessings.

A few minutes later, I felt the fairies come into me. My body moved with the waves of sensual energy and out of my mouth came involuntary coos and laughter. Sasha was taken completely by surprise and I could feel her embarrassment and discomfort. She murmured, "Oh my God, Shonagh! All the neighbors are going to hear you! Maybe I should leave the tent." She asked, incredulous, "Are you having orgasms?"

I answered through the fairy sounds, which was not as easy as I thought, "It's the fairies. I told you they'd come. It's okay, they're friendly."

A few minutes later they passed and I lay there smiling from ear to ear. "Well, I guess the medicine's kicked in after all!"

"Holy shit, Shonagh!"

"Honey, I tried to tell you. I think it's one thing for me to tell someone about this. It's quite another for them to actually experience it. It's pretty wild. They're very blissed out, sensual beings and very playful. It's all good, Sasha."

The frogs began to sing and in came the fairies again. Sasha started to roll with it and surprised me by engaging them. She asked, "Carly has been sick for awhile. What's wrong with her?"

I felt myself sink downward into the fairy realms with her question, and out of my mouth came the word, "Parasite!"

I heard Sasha say, "Of course!! That makes perfect sense!"

Then I said the word, "Purgative!"

"Okay. She needs some kind of purgative to get it out—who should I take her to?"

Again, without a thought, out of my mouth came, "Gerstmar! He's a wizard!" This was my naturopath and he was a brilliant doctor. Clearly the fairies understood his gifts. I could feel their delight when his name came through me.

The fairies passed out of my body and I began to feel a large spirit come into me. All of a sudden, my hands contorted into mudras that were talons. My arms opened and bent like wings. The frogs began singing and out of my mouth came a bird language. It was an owl but I wasn't making a "hoo" sound. I can't even begin to describe the sound, but I understood it to be a bird spirit song.

Again, I heard Sasha say something like, "What the fuck?" The spirit stayed in me for a few minutes and then passed.

I looked out the window of the tent and said, "My God. That was an owl. There must be a very large owl nearby. What grace, that was incredible." I said a thank-you to that spirit for singing through me.

The next thing I felt was a grandmother coming into me. Sasha made some negative comment about herself and the grandmother chastised her, practically crying, saying, "Sister of Light, do NOT talk about yourself in that way! You must NOT berate yourself like that anymore. That is an old spell, how you think of yourself. It goes now!" My arms began waving methodically as she spoke authoritatively through me, saying, "I cast it out! I cast it out! I cast it out! It is no more!"

Again Sasha engaged me, asking about her brother. She probed, "Isn't there something we can do for him? My mother is going to be a mess if he dies. She's not going to be able to handle it at all."

The grandmother answered through me, "Ah, sweet Sasha, there it is. You take responsibility for everyone's pain and you do not allow your own to come forward. You have taken on your mother's pain. You have done so since you were a child. She never meant for you to take it on but you were a sensitive soul and you took on the responsibility of her inner anguish. Her pain is not your responsibility. It does not belong to you. Let that go now."

I had my hand over her heart chakra and said, "Your brother will feel your love through the thick mists of his illness. When he goes, you will support your mother but you will feel your own pain, so old and heavy."

Then a force came into me that was enormous. Again, my hands curled into mudras of talons, my arms bent like wings, and my body began to spasm. This was a totally different frequency from that of the owl.

Sasha looked at me and said, "Holy FUCK!! You're a BIRD!!"

An otherworldly voice, not my own, cried out loud, "Eagle," and said to her, "You are Eagle Clan Sister. Your brother will die soon. The eagle waits for him to fly his spirit into the light. He has taken on a dark curse in this lifetime. He did this to protect you, Sister of the Light. He is ready to go soon and the curse will die with him. When the eagle takes his spirit to the light, no harm will follow him. He is a great warrior of light."

At that, Sasha sat up and reached for her phone and said, "I'm gonna call him."

The Eagle spirit laughed and said, "You cannot reach him in that way. In waking consciousness he is weak and failing, but do not underestimate the power of his spirit. These are larger realities, Sister Eagle. You must know what is beneath the surface of your perceptions. He took on this curse to your clan, so you could seed this Earth with your light. He will have earned his death when it comes."

Sasha then shared, "Oh my God. There is a family of eagles that nest on a tree next to my parents' house. We always see them."

Sasha then turned away from me, upset by the confirmation of her brother's looming death and the agonizing thought of her parents, bereft and broken by the loss of their son. I felt the Eagle spirit recede. In that moment,

Mother Earth came into me luminous, full of goddess light and love. My eyes were open and my hands were on Sasha's back. I saw them as liquid light with a glorious light radiating above our heads.

Mother Earth then spoke to Sasha and said, "Daughter of the Light, you must be that light now. Know yourself in this moment. You are a vast being with great gifts. You are our drummer. When you drum, you bring in the spirits. You drum them in. Now, you must know yourself. You came tonight to seek the truth—to know who you are. You have initiated the help of a high healer. You surround yourself with master adepts. You are very wise. Listen now. No more underestimating yourself. You must play a new beat on your drums now, Daughter. Play a new beat for us."

Then the eagle came back into me. Again my hands contorted into talons and my arms bent. Strange breathing sounds came from my mouth. I could feel Sasha was a little freaked out and to her credit, she kept it together very well.

The eagle told her, "Your brother was your husband in a lifetime where you lived in the teepee. Shonagh was your medicine sister—you grew up together. Your beloved left to go into battle. You begged him not to go but he went, and never came back. Your grief fractured you and you lost the daughter you were carrying in your womb. It is your niece, Gabriela, the one you are close to in this life. When your brother goes and Gabriela loses her father, she will need you. You are her torchbearer, Sister of the Light. She will go through a dark time and you will guide her to the other side."

Sasha heard all of this and whispered, "He was my husband in another life? Gabriela was our child? That is so wild! No wonder I'm so close to her."

At this, Sasha began asking questions. She was still sharing a house with her ex-girlfriend and she'd wanted to fix it up as she thought she'd be there another year. She asked, "Should I remodel the kitchen? I want to make a nicer home for my girls."

Eagle responded, "Do nothing. You will achieve success in your work. Money is coming to you. You will find your own place to nest and your Gabriela will be coming to live with you for a time."

Sasha filled with joy and said, "Yay! I would love that." Then she asked about her beloved Alexis. "What about Alexis? What's going to happen with us?"

Eagle answered, "Eagle Sister, she is going to break open your heart. She is caught up in the spell. The shell around her is very thick and she is not pecking very hard to leave it."

"She sits like this." I sat up and crossed my arms defiantly over my chest, all the while, my hands still curled into talons.

"She thinks she is right and her Sasha is wrong. Yet in her heart, she loves you so very much. You must shift the roles you have played together. She is not your mother and you are not her daughter. She can be difficult to reach, but you will reach her through your open heart. It must break first, though, Sister Eagle. You will not like it, but it will serve you."

Sasha began to speak in a self-deprecating tone again. I put my hands over her heart and my face close to her ear whispering, "Listen, Sister of Light. These spirits are not going to leave until you get this piece, and I'm getting tired, so please get it through your Sasha-head that you are EAGLE CLAN SISTER OF LIGHT! No more berating yourself, my Sasha!"

She sighed and said, "All right, I get it. I get it." I felt it penetrate and I sat back up.

Then White Owl came into me and I became her, feeling more fluid with her energy in me compared to the eagle. The energies were distinctly different. As White Owl, I said to Sasha, "We are clan sisters. You are Eagle Clan. I am White Owl clan. We have come in, Sister Eagle. We came in under the radar. We have responded to Mother Earth's call and we are here to reclaim our lands. We are everywhere now. They have made the sacred medicine illegal because it opens the channels to Spirit. Our channels to Spirit were disrupted many thousands of years ago by beings not of this Earth. They hold a dark claw around this planet that has been in place since that time. We are calling back our sovereignty and ushering in the age of Light. The bird clans are here, Sister Eagle. We are here!"

I brushed my cheek against the white owl fan hanging from the ceiling. Sasha was sitting up looking at me and said, "Shonagh, you are so absolutely beautiful right now. Your face and your hair—you look beautiful."

"I am White Owl, Sasha." I sat gently moving my torso in slow circular motions. We sat in silence for a few minutes, then Sasha left for the bathroom.

"Good, honey. Go pee. You have received a 'healing-maximus' tonight."

"I feel completely different," Sasha said.

Out of my mouth came the words, "You will leave my teepee forever changed."

I lay down alone and immediately thought of my dad, who was dying. I knew years ago that he would leave before my mother, and last year it came to me that his time was near.

Early in the year they found a tumor in his brain and his lung. Brain surgery followed and I knew my father lacked the strength for such an ordeal. The devil's brew of pharmaceuticals they pumped into him sent my father's fragile body right over the edge. A few days earlier, my mother phoned to say he was going into hospice care.

I did not want to see my father in that way. I had decided to go for the funeral, but I could not face him in his suffering. As I lay in the tent, White Owl told me my dad was requesting my medicine. He wanted me to come and help him die. I began to sob. I knew how to initiate shamanic death rites and it felt to me he was asking me to do that for him. His spirit was sick of the crazy-making hospital medicine. He wanted to be released.

I was told to bring my mesa and an eagle feather. I asked, "Why an eagle feather?" White Owl told me my father's lineage of many lifetimes was Eagle Clan. In this lifetime, I was the eldest of his four adopted children. I was told that our soul agreement was that he would raise me, and one of my gifts to him would be to help him die.

Sasha returned to the tent and rushed inside to hold me. I shared with her through my sobs what I'd been told. I was to leave Memorial Day weekend, which was a few days away. I would stay for a week but White Owl said it might be longer. Sasha hugged me and said she would be here for me. I felt so close to her. I had been shown a glimpse of her essence and I was deeply touched by the beauty of her being. I was graced to have her as my dear friend.

We talked for a while longer and then attempted to settle in to sleep. Sleep wouldn't come, however, as I could not get comfortable. I could feel Sasha beside me and I could tell she wasn't fully asleep. White Owl spoke to me and told me the reason she couldn't sleep outside was because of her lifetime in the teepee.

When her beloved died in battle, her grief never left her. She spent long nights in her teepee grieving him until she died.

I woke Sasha from her half-sleep and told her I knew why she couldn't sleep outside. I roused us from our tent and we headed inside to sleep in the comfort of the guest room.

The following morning after just a few hours of sleep, I knew I needed to book a ticket to Tucson. I found Richard in the kitchen and asked if he would please book round-trip tickets using his air miles. He asked when, and when I told him it was in a few days he said, "That's Memorial Day weekend, Shonagh. Everything is going to be booked already."

"Well, Spirit told me I'm going next weekend, so let's just take a look and see what's available." Sure enough, he found a direct flight for me on Thursday with just three seats left. Spirit had also told me I might be staying longer than a week. I had him book my return flight for the following Wednesday and interestingly enough, Richard said that the flight back was overbooked and I'd have to get to the airport early to fight for a seat.

"Hmmmm," I thought. "We'll see what's up with that." I made a mental note to pack a black dress just in case. I would listen for guidance from Spirit as to how to proceed as I went along.

I was now understanding that the form of shamanism I had been guided to was one in which I would engage the sacred medicine and allow myself to be possessed by helping spirits. The word *possessed* has negative connotations, but I understood that I was a conduit for a specific frequency of energies that had agreed to work with me prior to my incarnating.

I trusted these beings. They never told me what to do. They had no ill intent and they never stayed in my body beyond the encounter. They were benevolent beings, and

I understood that our relationship extended far beyond the confines of this time-space continuum. I was deeply humbled by their presence and eager to work with them in service for the greater good. I felt graced that I was able to touch into such wondrous energies.

I thought about the possibility of bringing them through in a group setting and was told, "This is not parlor tricks." I got that there would be specific people who I would share this experience with in the future. They would be "those with eyes to see and ears to hear." I would go into shamanic trance state and bring through the beings most appropriate for the needs of that person or group. This would be part of my service to others, offering them healing and guidance in this very unusual and profound way.

This was a part of the shaman's path. Traditional shamans worked with plant medicines to bring forth healing for tribe members. We certainly could use this kind of healing in our culture. It seems strange to the average person only because there is no reference point in our society for this level of spiritual healing. I have had to find my own way to this for that very reason. I know I have been divinely guided and I am in my dharma. It is my hope that more people will open their hearts to shamanic healing and the spirit world. I know that Sasha will never forget our night together and I know she is forever changed. This is the power of this medicine and I am ever grateful for the experience.

⁓ 26 ⁓

Solo Flight

The leaves will fall and become the ground
and lonely songs are the only sound
when you're all done growing up
you get off the carousel of illusion
 catch a leaf and make a wish
spin the dial part the mist
open up and let love in . . .

—Sasha

I arrived in Tucson, emotionally prepared to see my dying father. Once there, I felt an inner strength I didn't have a year ago. At that time I would have crumbled at the site of my dad, swollen-faced and desperately thin from the horrible side effects of all the drugs they were feeding him. I was able to put aside my reaction and access only my love and compassion, enabling me to better serve him.

Before leaving for the hospital, I laid out my mesa and rattle to take with me. I placed the eagle feather on the mesa and gathered up my purse. My mother saw the feather and asked, "Is that our eagle feather?"

I wasn't sure I'd heard her correctly and asked her what she meant. She told me they had an eagle feather they'd found on an island in Canada. It was kept in the guest room where my father would often sleep, stored inside the TV cabinet. I followed my mother into the room and she pulled a large and very beautiful eagle feather out from a drawer. What were the odds that my parents would have an eagle feather, of all things? I was learning not to doubt my experiences with the spirits. They were piercing the veils around me, speaking through synchronicity at every turn.

Over the next few days I visited my father, keeping him company and working on him energetically. At one point his doctor came into the room and my father introduced me with pride, saying, "This is my daughter, Shonagh. She's a shaman and she's working her magic on me." He said it with such sincerity I could have cried. I was past looking to my parents for acknowledgment and I realized in that moment I was receiving that from him.

My father was not the most emotionally available person, and at the same time, I knew he loved me very much. When I was growing up he was drinking daily. As a teenager I was mostly embarrassed for him. He was definitely not someone I looked to for counsel. We didn't have much of a relationship until I was in my twenties. By then he was sober, and for a while we were very close. Over the ensuing years we drifted apart somewhat, although I always knew I could come to him with anything; he never judged me. He had a dry sense of humor that brought levity to even the most serious situations.

A persistent phrase had been haunting me for the past few weeks—"the death of the old masculine." Every time I thought of my father dying, that line came into my head. How interesting, that after the intensity of the past few months, where I'd let go of the major masculine players in my life, it would culminate in the ensuing death of my father. I cried at the thought of this. At the same time it felt almost scripted and weirdly perfect. A pattern was completing itself.

In a way, my father's death would mark the end of my old patterns of relating to the masculine. When a parent dies, on some level they set their progeny free. I felt this energetically, as if a cord was unhooking from me. I understood it to be the announcement of a whole new beginning, standing alone as a woman at this pivotal time in my life.

With so many medicine journeys behind me, and with the intense soul searching I'd done, it felt like I'd burned away multiple layers of my old self. I knew I would be guided and held as I moved forward. This was not a naïve hope, but a deep knowing. It filled me with a calm resolve to greet my independence with confidence and grace. I felt the present moment was rich with possibilities. I had turned my pain into medicine through the writing of this book. My teaching, too, had deepened through that pain. I was ready to take myself to the next level of service, putting my voice out to the collective through writing and public speaking.

Today, my community of friends is very dear to me and I will continue to cultivate that. I have a sense that at this time in our history, community is imperative. If we want to shift to a culture of consciousness, it will depend on the development of communities that model a spirit of "power with" rather than "power over." I'm aware of a variety of communities—spiritual, food/farming, artistic—cropping up around the country. These communities embrace a spirit of cooperation, working together with integrity.

I know these communities are fueled by the shifting consciousness that is showering our planet at this time. I often say that the spiritual awakening so many people are experiencing right now is the biggest news you'll never hear. I have noticed a growing hunger in both men and women for a deeper experience, a connection to something that holds true meaning. I have made a commitment to inspire other women to create their own communities to gather in a sacred manner and remember to be sisters, mentors, and elders.

With so many books on how to find one's soul mate, it occurs to me that this book is about finding one's own soul. I have an expanded experience of myself now, and my "I" has moved far beyond the personality called "Shonagh." I have discovered that this "I" can navigate through untold realms and engage with spirits that offer guidance and wisdom. I am greatly enhanced by my relationship with Spirit and *Self*—and I'm ever deepened.

If more people could or would venture into themselves and open their consciousness in this way, I believe our culture could and would change dramatically. I have no doubt that depression could be reduced exponentially. The aimless, bored, or jaded could be awakened to a whole new awareness that could have a profound impact, imbuing their lives with meaning.

The journey into Self and the experience of connecting with Spirit through the entheogens is beyond anything I can convey. It gifts one with a true paradigm shift going beyond what any book, film, or person can describe—it *must* be experienced. When one touches the sacred within oneself, it opens up realms of infinite possibility that beckon to be explored. One has the experience of oneself as a quantum being with a realization of how limited the life journey has been up to this point.

There is much to be explored with the use of these sacred plant medicines. Terence McKenna talked about

g into these realms and bringing back ideas. We can't
: our problems with the same mindset that created
them. The medicine opens consciousness, which opens
the mind to a larger paradigm. If great numbers of people
engaged entheogens—with reverence and care—there is
a good chance that some solutions to our pressing problems could be found as a result of the mind-expansion
these medicines induce.

For myself, my interior shift has been life changing. I
know as a daughter of Spirit, that I am loved and cherished by beautiful beings of light. For someone who had
predicated her worthiness on being loved by a mate, this is
no small awareness. I have felt my own luminous light on
this medicine and I value myself in ways that I never have
before. I have seen dimensions of my being through these
journeys that has inspired a level of compassion and love
for myself—something that I have never felt in the past.

My life looms before me, not as something I'm fearful
of, but rather as an invitation to fully express the gifts that
I have come here to share. Soon I will be packing up my
beautiful daughters, along with our coterie of animals and
two very vibrant beehives, and moving into a little country cottage. I relish the thought of truly being on my own.
I will make my living doing what I cherish—working with
medicine women.

Recently I awoke with this beautiful image—seeing
myself walking alone toward a golden sunrise. On my back
were two of the most exquisite white wings—of such size
and power that I knew there was no place they couldn't
take me. I end this chapter with that lovely vision. Myself
as a woman deepened and greatly resourced.

My wings ready for flight.

❧ 27 ❧

Musings

Extending cognitive studies into the phenomenology of psychotherapy, Grob (2007) has shown that beneficially reframing death anxiety can occur with psilocybin, and Mithoefer, (2007) that MDMA-assisted psychotherapy can reduce Post Traumatic Stress Disorder in patients who have been intractable to other treatments. Other clinical leads suggest treating cluster headaches, obsessive-compulsive disorder, neuroses and psychosis, alcohol and addiction (Winkelman and Roberts, 2007). Except for cluster headaches, the cures are usually correlated with mystical experiences. What phenomenological shifts during mystical experiences reframe thoughts, emotions and identity so much that they apparently often cure anxiety, post-traumatic stress disorder, and addictions and alcoholism? ... For cognitive scientists who want to study higher order processes experimentally, psychedelics provide a ready lead.
—Thomas B. Roberts, Ph.D. Article: *Enhancing Cognition, Intelligence, and the Cognitive Sciences with Psychedelics.* Printed with permission by Dr. Roberts.

Recently, one of my friends asked me what is the greatest gift I've received from the mushroom medicine. I couldn't give her just one answer, as so much has shifted within me as a result of my explorations. I told her that I trust Spirit implicitly now. I said that because of my direct experience with the logos on the medicine, I know I am *never* alone. I told her of my absolute knowing that I am connected to something rich and profoundly mysterious. This is not something I "believe." I *know* it because I've *experienced* connection with the sacred.

This has deepened my appreciation for the gift of life. It has made me more self-aware, enhancing my relationships as well as my teaching. Working with the medicine has magnified my intuition and given me tremendous insight into the world I live in. It is as if the veils around me have been removed. All of this because of my tenacious explorations with entheogenic mushrooms. I could have elaborated even further, but my friend got the point.

That being said, I recommend some deep self-reflection before engaging the mushrooms. I had eight years of focused psycho-spiritual work under my belt before entering these realms. Terence McKenna once warned that those who wish to avoid looking at certain things should stay away from this medicine. The fact is that the mushrooms amplify the deep psyche, both the conscious and unconscious minds. Any negative habits or behaviors you have are brought to your awareness, as are any personal conflicts you may be experiencing. The beauty is that the awareness of such can be a powerful trigger for positive change in personal growth and in the way we engage others. The mushrooms will open your consciousness to ways in which you can create positive shift in your life. People in our culture are in desperate need of this.

There is anthropological research that shows how various cultures around the world were affected by the use of entheogens. These medicines were not profaned as they have been in Western culture. They were regarded as windows to Spirit and were used ceremonially with great reverence and respect. Marlene Dobkin de Rios discusses this in her book, *Hallucinogens: Cross-Cultural Perspectives*. Dobkin de Rios studied eleven societies from the Americas to New Guinea. Each of these societies consistently worked with entheogenic substances. Dobkin de Rios notes that the use of these medicines has had a positive effect on the ethical and moral systems of these cultures.

In Tshogana Tsonga society in Mozambique, adolescent girls are initiated with an entheogen called *Datura fatuosa*. The entheogen brings them into union with the fertility god and adds a sacred element to the formal ritual of welcoming them into womanhood. Unlike our society, which sends many of its adolescent girls into a cycle of self-loathing, this culture produces women who are inducted as a group into a sacred ceremonial rite that bonds the initiates and welcomes them as integral members of their community.

In the South American rainforests, an entheogen called Ayahuasca is used in a group ritual. The shaman or *ayahuasquero* brews a combination of *Banisteriopsis* species that make for a powerful psychedelic experience. The ayahuasquero and the participants drink the brew, which confers deep healing in those who ingest it. These cultures use the medicine for a variety of reasons. Before going to battle, warriors ingested Ayahuasca in sacred ceremony. It was also used by hunters to locate the position of animals. The spirit of the Ayahuasca can reveal both the cause of an illness and the remedy for it. It could also be used for the eradication of possessing spirits, black magic and curses. Large corporate interests have decimated most of these Amazonian cultures, their traditions further eroded by zealous missionaries. The very few remaining indigenous societies maintain close social structures and continue to work with this profound medicine.

The inclusion of ritual that accompanies the ingestion of these entheogenic substances is highly important. The plant medicines are not used as an escape mechanism. They offer members of the community a deeper sense of belonging. Plant medicines were used for diagnosis and healing, connecting to the spirit realms, oracular guidance, and sacred group experiences. Ritual elevates the entire experience and instills a level of respect for the entheogens.

It's appalling that here in the United States, psilocybin is categorized in the same class as dangerous street drugs like heroin. This was a drastic overreaction to the '60s counterculture, where Timothy Leary's cry to "Turn on, tune in, drop out" threatened the status quo and terrified the old guard. At that time psilocybin was still legal, having been thrust into the culture's awareness for just thirteen years as a result of Gordon Wasson's 1957 *Life Magazine* article about mushroom curandera, Doa Maria Sabina. Leary, who taught at Harvard at the time, had conducted some compelling experiments that showed both psilocybin and LSD to have potentially positive effects in the area of psychotherapy.

One investigation in particular was called the Marsh Chapel Experiment. This took place at Boston University Chapel, where twenty theology students participated. Half were given psilocybin in pill form; the other half were given a placebo. Leary's team of researchers later had the subjects fill out a questionnaire about their experiences.

Afterward, a group of researchers examined specific parts of the questionnaire where the subjects had detailed their mystical experiences. They then compared these to mystical passages of illumined revelations taken from various sacred texts.

Not surprising to anyone familiar with mushrooms, the subjects who were given the psilocybin had mystical experiences on par with the mystics of old, whose accounts could be found in sacred religious books. This had profound implications. It created a potential threat to the religious elite who had been posing as the intermediaries to God for the past two thousand years. Here was evidence that one could bypass the dogma and dictums of our state-approved religions and experience the sacred firsthand.

Shamanic communities have been working with entheogenic substances as far back as time can tell. These communities have been systematically decimated by organized religion for many centuries now. Various sects of Christianity have been infiltrating traditional communities around the world to proselytize and turn them away from their traditions. The shaman is demonized, along with the medicines they work with. In the book, *Shamanism and Tantra in the Himalayas*, by Claudia Muller-Ebeling, Christian Ratsch, and Surendra Bahadur Shahi, the authors discuss a Jesuit "Father" they once knew who lived in Kathmandu and Patan for a number of years. This Jesuit wrote a book on shamanism called *Faith Healers of the Himalayas*. The authors of *Shamanism and Tantra* note that shamanism actually has nothing to do with faith. Shamanism is about direct experience. Religion requires faith because it lacks experience.

The author asked this man what a Jesuit has to do with shamanism. The Jesuit responded that he was on "assignment" from his superiors to examine shamanism to the point where it could then be infiltrated and undermined by the Church. This story is fairly recent. The attacks on this practice have never ceased. The threat is clear. Shamanism, with its use of sacred entheogens, provides direct engagement with the realms of Spirit. In the words of Comanche Chief Quanah Parker, "The white man goes into his church house and talks *about* Jesus, but the Indian goes into his teepee and talks *to* Jesus."

Controlled studies on subjects taking entheogens have shown that they provide a person with an expanded understanding of themselves and their place in the universe. The substances have the power to shift these people more deeply than anything they've experienced thus far.

An article in the Sunday *New York Times Magazine* (April 2012), written by Lauren Slater, discussed the use of psilocybin for terminally ill patients. A small study was being conducted at Harbor U.C.L.A. Medical Center by psychiatrists and researchers. Psilocybin was administered to twelve recipients to see if it would reduce their fear of death. This was a double blind study, where a placebo was used, and neither the researchers nor the participants would know what they were given. The results of the study were published in 2008 in the *Archives of General Psychiatry*. The researchers found that psilocybin markedly reduced the anxiety and depression the subjects had felt around their looming death.

It is important to note that not all psychiatric experiments with psychotropic substances have been ethical. There is room for abuse, and elements within both the psychiatric community and the military have committed egregious wrongs.

In Scott Noble's brilliant documentary, *Human Resources*, Dr. Colin Ross discusses the appalling research done on children by Dr. Lauretta Bender. Dr. Bender was a revered child neuropsychiatrist famous for developing the Bender-Gestalt test, which is a widely used test to determine visual motor maturity. Dr. Bender conducted horrific experiments on children as young as five, who were given hallucinogens like LSD for days, weeks, months, and sometimes years in a row. Her work was published in peer-reviewed literature and upon her death she was given a full-page obituary in the *Journal of Psychiatric Medicine*. Her colleagues never reported her and there was no outrage expressed over her published work, which detailed her experiments.

The military, too, has its dark history with hallucinogens. The documentary explores how the military conducted experiments with LSD and mescaline on unsuspecting soldiers. In addition, a vast collection of information and documents concerning the C.I.A.'s covert role with psychedelics has been amassed by researcher Jan Irvin. This information can be found on his website, *www.gnosticmedia.com*.

To sum this piece: Plant medicine belongs to *we the people*, the citizens of Earth. It must not be kept within the confines of any medical or governmental entity. Those sectors of our society that use this medicine for experimentation must be held to the highest ethics. Plant medicine is a sacred sacrament that gifts the user with an expanded consciousness. To use it for manipulation and harm is a despicable, depraved act of malice.

Thomas B. Roberts, Ph,D, is professor emeritus at Northern Illinois University. He teaches a course called Foundation of Psychedelic Studies, which is the only college course of its kind. He is the author of the books, *Psychedelic Horizons, The Psychedelic Future of the Mind: How Entheogens Are Enhancing Cognition, Boosting Intelligence, and Raising Values,* and editor of *Psychoactive Sacramentals: Essays on Entheogens and Religion.* In *Psychedelic Horizons,* he discusses the mind and how we are trained to develop the ordinary awake state, without the realization of the vast sea of other "mindbody" states available to us.

As these other mind-body states remain unexplored, our mind is likened to a computer that is only used to play a chess game, while the plethora of other programs remain unused. Dr. Roberts states that we are hindering ourselves and our children, and ultimately our future, by focusing exclusively on one state of awareness, the cognitive processing area of the brain. Our mind is a multi-state organism and it is time now to learn to access its full capacity rather than continue to stay in mental limitation.

Dr. Roberts points out that sleep and dreaming are also mind states, and if we do not access those states, our ability to function in the ordinary awake state will crash and burn. He wonders if other mind-body states work cohesively together to strengthen and support each other. It is a fact that people who practice other forms of concentration, such as martial arts and meditation, find that their awake states are enhanced as a result. Dr. Roberts calls for more research into how different mind states communicate and affect each other.

Ingesting entheogens like psilocybin will open the multi-state doors within the mind and offer access to untapped areas of consciousness. Terence McKenna once said that what this world desperately needs is consciousness. When one taps these mind states, new ideas come in. The boundaries within the mind have been lifted and the user is opened to new insights and perspectives. This is an enormous complement to our normal awake state because it has now been enhanced by a greater awareness, which the user did not previously have. Dr. Roberts says, "My psychedelic colleagues and I have found that once we started thinking with a multistate view, the old single-state paradigm fades to gray. I don't at all think it's an exaggeration to say that for me experiencing psychedelics and following up the intellectual avenues they pointed toward were at least the equivalent of earning my Doctorate at Stanford."

There are other mind-state activities that will contribute to expanding consciousness such as meditation, hypnosis, sound therapy, and breath work, to name a few. Entheogens have the advantage of getting you there considerably quicker, and shamans understand this very well. Roberts says we have multiple mind states, anywhere from hundreds to thousands that remain dormant. Shamans use both psychoactive plants as well as the monotonous sounds of drums or rattles to alter the brain and bring themselves into connection with these mind states.

A noticeable occurrence that results from the use of entheogens is the enhancement of "moral sense and intuition." Dr. Roberts notes that when someone leaves their personal identity mind state to experience a transpersonal mind state, the "I" dissolves, bringing one into connection with "other." This enhances the internal guidance system or intuition, as the "I" has been removed and the "logos" has been accessed, opening the traveler to a larger sense of knowing. I myself have experienced this from my journeys with the sacred mushrooms. My intuition is stronger and clearer than it has ever been, and my desire to be in service has never been more heartfelt.

Entheogens are a powerful pathway to enlightenment. I realize that is irritating to certain people who have dedicated their lives to their guru and spend considerable time every day meditating and chanting. Terence McKenna once said that you can spend the next fifteen years sweeping the floors of the ashram in the hopes of receiving that one truth you've been waiting for from the lips of your guru, or you could take those five grams of psilocybin you have sitting in your fridge. Not to say that meditation isn't useful, because I do it myself on a regular basis, and there certainly are some gurus out there who are indeed enlightened. At the same time, a wondrously rich landscape of consciousness awaits those who choose to journey with sacred plant medicines. The experience of such is highly enlightening and will continue to expand the seeker exponentially.

Clark Heinrich, who wrote *Magic Mushrooms in Religion and Alchemy*, tells the story of what really happened when Ram Dass gave LSD to his guru, Neem Karoli Baba. Heinrich, a longtime student of yoga and Eastern spirituality, studied with a teacher who was once this guru's right-hand man, having built and run five of his ashrams. This teacher told Heinrich that when Ram Dass handed the guru three tablets containing 305 micrograms each, the guru palmed the LSD and only swallowed air.

Heinrich writes, "Many Indian gurus are adept at sleight of hand and small magic tricks, and are not always above using a little subterfuge 'for the good of the disciple.' But the story doesn't end with palming the LSD. The guru later ground the tablets into powder and mixed it with a little of the fine white ash from his sacred fire. This he then gave to two unsuspecting disciples who had been visiting from a distant place and were now departing. Ash from a guru's fire is considered Prasad and yes, it is eaten. I don't know anything of the men's journey home, but it was probably quite eventful, especially considering the Himalayan roads, and filled with wondrous exclamations about the guru's tremendous powers."

Some who have dedicated themselves to specific spiritual practices feel the entheogenic path is "cheating." Unfortunately, those who consider their spiritual practice to be more "legitimate" or "pure" have consistently dismissed psychoactive substances. I am inclined to follow the shamanic path, the oldest spirituality in the world—a non-hierarchical path that recognizes Spirit in every living thing, animate and inanimate. It's a path that embraces the sacred plants, approaching them with respect, honoring, and with a heart that is open to the experience of *unio mystica*.

A shaman is quoted in *Shamanism and Tantra in the Himalayas* as saying that they *learn* when they enter a high trance state. In that place they feel the connection to the repository of knowledge that is held in the memory of all mankind. I believe that what is stored in the memory of all mankind is the knowledge of our connection to the Divine, our knowing of ourselves as Children of Light. Divine truths are revealed through the respectful use of entheogenic medicine. It is my prayer that these sacred plants weave through our broken culture like mycelium, making themselves available to all who seek their sacred wisdom.

Epilogue

Star Beings

In fact, there did not seem to be any limit to what Grof's LSD subjects could tap into. In an even stranger vein, they sometimes encountered nonhuman intelligences during their cerebral travels, discarnate beings, spirit guides from "higher planes of consciousness," and other suprahuman entities.
—Michael Talbot, *The Holographic Universe*

This book ends with an interesting development in my medicine journeys. June 5, 2012 was the date of an astronomical event that many people in my community were buzzing about. Venus was to conjunct the sun that day, after an eight-year transit. During that transit, the planet Venus follows a path that is in the shape of a five-pointed star. The sun conjunction was akin to a sacred union of opposites. In this case, the sun represents the solar male/masculine heart of the universe and Venus is the goddess of love. From an esoteric viewpoint, this sacred union would result in a cosmic orgasm of energy that would be felt throughout our universe.

I had a feeling that this was a much larger event than people realized. It felt like a huge portal was being opened. I knew of a number of people who'd planned to watch the event in the sky during the few hours it would be occurring. Others were participating in sacred ritual around this event. It came to me to do the medicine that evening in an endeavor to go through that portal. I called and invited my friend, Amelia, who by now was my official co-pilot in these explorations. She readily agreed that this was an opportunity not to be missed.

We set up my tent on the little island. Amelia took a small dose of the medicine and I ate six grams. We lay down in our tent and waited for the medicine to take effect. After an hour or so the medicine kicked in and to my amazement, I felt myself in the stars, watching Venus move across the sun in a blaze of violet light. It was indescribably beautiful. I shared my experience with Amelia and was stunned to hear she'd experienced the same thing. Then I felt a rush of energy coming into my body. It was the strongest energetic vibration I'd ever felt. I opened my mouth to speak and out came these words, with great mirth, "They've got their guns pointed and their radar on and yet here we are! In a tiny tent in Redmond!" Then I turned my face to Amelia and my voice said, "Waste of money, don't you think?" We both broke out in laughter.

My voice was very different and the energy speaking through me presented itself as a group of beings. They addressed us as "daughters of Mu" (short for Lemuria) and were delighted to be in our company. They referred to our earlier shared experience, saying, "The daughters of Mu had front row seats! Big sister Venus conjuncted her lover, sun! You wouldn't have missed that one! Get ready for everything to change now, daughters of Mu!" I knew right away these were star beings. I would describe them as someone who is incredibly smart, really funny, and has had a few cocktails. They had us laughing throughout the evening and they talked to us like they were addressing old friends.

Amelia and I were planning to leave for Ashland in a couple of days to join a group of priestesses for an intensive taught by a master teacher. She was a PhD scholar of the ancient priestesshoods of the Mediterranean. We would be doing high ritual together and learning about these sacred women.

The star beings addressed this upcoming weekend by saying, "Oh, they won't like what you girls will be doing this weekend! They won't like it at all! You will be creating *big* geometries!" The "they" the beings were referring to were the shadow forces that have been running the show on this planet for a long time. The star beings seemed almost mocking of them. They told us we were entering a time where we would be able to access a high level of magic that had been taken from us a long time ago.

They then turned their attention to Amelia and spoke of the depth of her work as a midwife/healer. They did not want her to underestimate the impact of what she was bringing through with her healing. They explained that she often worked behind the scenes when she incarnated, working quietly yet powerfully. Then they said of me, "This one . . . not so quiet!" Both Amelia and I laughed at that one. They called me their "clarion" and informed me that this book would touch hearts. They told us, "You are awaking as if from a dream, and you will remember every detail."

They talked to us about frequencies, saying that each person carries a specific frequency. They explained that the more work we do on *ourselves*, to clear our old stuff and attune to our hearts, the stronger our frequencies become. They also advised us to clear our minds of the

ivel" we'd been told to believe our whole lives. They
d that our minds had been abused in the worst way,
__ d by seeing through the façade of our artificial cultural
constructs, we would free ourselves from the dream.

The beings said that we are like generators and the
more awake we are, the more powerful our frequencies.
This affects others in a way that enables them to awaken.
This was likened to the tipping point, where enough people come into a particular body of knowledge and all of a
sudden everyone seems to know it. The same is true here.
The frequencies we generate can be felt by other people,
and also by the natural world around us. If we are radiating a frequency that is heart-centered and clear, it shifts
the surrounding energy. If everyone is in a frequency of
fear and chaos, it colors the way people think and act and
it affects the environment as well.

The beings were very clear about the importance of
tuning into our hearts. Amelia and I understood this well.
Amelia's work was all about the heart center. I'd created
the foundation of my teaching on the heart as well. My
teacher, Brugh Joy, taught heart-centered awareness and
was called by some the "heart priest." We both had the
sense that we were being activated in some way by these
beings. The mood of the evening was raucous and fun and
we laughed for hours. They delivered to us their messages
with such wit. The frequency of joy in the tent was very
palpable and it felt like it was taking place in an entirely
different dimension.

When the beings finally bade us farewell, we retired
to the house, ebullient over our experience. I exclaimed,
"Holy shit! Those were star beings! They were so FUN! I
had no idea I could connect to that energy!" We couldn't
fall asleep right away, as the excitement was too great.

The following day we speculated about these star beings. I had heard Barbara Marciniak channel the Pleiadians a couple of times several years ago. I said that they seemed very similar to those beings. I kept feeling that that was indeed what had come in.

A couple of days later, Amelia and I made the eight-hour drive to Ashland to work with an impressive group of priestesses. Before we left, I understood that I was to bring my medicine. I balked and said to my guidance, "But I just did a big dose two days ago!" I was told to trust the guidance and so I did.

On Friday we found ourselves in a beautiful temple space sitting in circle with a very astute group of women. Our teacher began by sharing her research into the Greek mythologies, discussing in great detail the priestess cults that worshipped the various goddesses. Her focus was the oracles and the divine birth priestesses. The divine birth cults endeavored to engage the goddess on the astral realms in a very high tantric state. If they were lucky, parthenogenesis would occur and they would conceive a divine being that could not come through the normal sexual channels. Our guide had done scholarly research on this topic for many years and her work on the subject, although not widely known, was highly respected.

As she was sharing this information with us, I was having many "aha" moments, feeling a familiarity with various aspects of the material she was presenting. She mentioned that these ancient priestesses were working with the Pleiades in their rituals. I later shared with the group about the experience Amelia and I had had with the "star beings" two nights ago. At the break, the teacher and her friend, Ines, came to talk to me. Ines told me her husband had channeled the Pleiadians for a number of years and that by my description, she felt the beings that had come through me were Pleiadian. It came to me that I was to do the medicine the following night and bring them through for the group. I asked what they thought about it and they were very agreeable, saying they wanted to be there. I let the group know and said I would be doing this in the evening after dinner. I joked with them that these beings liked to party and might keep us up rather late.

That evening, around twelve women sat in the temple room. I lay on the floor and waited for what seemed an interminably long time for the medicine to kick in. At one point it was explained to me by my inner guides that they were preparing my matrix to receive the being that was coming in. I explained this to the group and they were content to wait it out.

After ninety minutes or so, I got up on my knees. I was holding a smudging fan made from a barn-owl tail in my right hand. I had the sensation of a very high-vibration being within me. "I" then receded as if in a dream, and the being, who felt feminine, came through for the next three hours or so. She proceeded to talk about frequencies, explaining that Lemuria was a frequency that was held on this planet for a certain period of time. She went on to discuss the infiltration of this planet by what she referred to as "schoolyard bullies" who essentially stripped us of our power and proceeded to run the planet on the frequencies of fear and chaos.

She answered a number of questions that various members of the group asked and then began working very deeply with certain people. She took them back to specific lifetimes where certain "geometries" were created that carried a particular theme through lifetimes until it was resolved. She proceeded to unwind the geometries while explaining the situation and the lessons around it. Her work with people went deep. She could see beneath their personalities into the depths of their essence and she held them with absolute love and reverence.

The evening had an otherworldly feel to it. I was told later that there was a very pronounced vibration of love and sweetness that everyone could feel. We were all bathed in the frequency that this being brought with her. Although I barely remember what was said through me, I was aware of being infused with what I would describe as particles or filaments of pure light. An interesting result from the evening was that an old injury I'd had in my right hip completely disappeared. For the past five months I'd had constant pain in my hip, yet I stubbornly exercised anyway, hoping it would subside. After that evening, it disappeared and has not returned.

The following day I woke up cracked wide open by the experience. I was very tired but also very blown away by what had occurred. At one point the previous evening, the being had revealed herself to be one of the seven sisters of the Pleiades. I could feel her in me still. My heart was open in such a way that I felt no attachment to any of my life stories. I was holding a heart frequency of such purity that I feared nothing. I felt myself as love and I saw everyone around me as fellow beings of light and beauty.

At the end of the class on Sunday, our teacher took time to discuss the events of the previous night. Her friend, Ines, spoke, telling me she'd been around channels for many years but never had she experienced a frequency of love like she had the previous night. Ines said that she'd known channels that had come close to that, but they could only hold the frequency for an hour or so. She looked at me and said, "Shonagh, you held that frequency for almost three hours!" She then thanked me for modeling the ancient oracles with humility and respect.

I realized in that moment I was being witnessed and affirmed. As courageous and outgoing as I am, I am plagued by self-doubt. I fight it constantly. I knew that this was a pivotal moment for me. I had been a quiet channel for a number of years. Years ago, a spiritual teacher told me that I was a channel and suggested that I channel in circle, bringing through wisdom and answering questions for the group. I was horrified. My exact words to her were, "No fucking way! I will sit in my room and I will write down what comes to me, but there is NO WAY I am going to sit in front of a bunch of people and channel!"

That afternoon, after Ines spoke, I felt the being come through me and began to read for the women in the circle who hadn't been there the night before. It was beautiful. The following day Amelia and I made the long drive home. I was in no shape to drive. I was still utterly cracked open. The beings explained to me on the ride home that it would take six days for the new frequencies to fully integrate within me. They also gave me a heads-up that "not everyone is going to like the new Shonagh." They said that for each person who turns their back, there would be many others with ears to hear.

My first week home was definitely different. My personality was noticeably altered for a few days. I was operating from a place of pure open-heartedness and joy. I had no defenses and felt no need for them. I was relating to people from a place of appreciation and wonder, delighting in the connection. Richard could not have been more accepting. He understood right away that I had touched something very profound, and he was delighted to hear that I was channeling these beings. That week I shed any and all of the story I'd held around my relationship with Richard. We turned a corner that week and have been close friends ever since.

I began to put it out that I was channeling and I hosted my first group gathering the week I got back. That evening I brought through a different being that was the spokesperson for a group of spirits that I could feel around me. She proceeded to give a teaching and answered a number of questions. The feel of the room was again very warm and loving. I understood that the frequency of the group or individual I was working with determined what beings would come through me.

I am careful about channeled material, as much of it feels like nonsense to me. After receiving a transmission I always review the message to see if it has any relevance. These beings I have connected with have thus far been very clear about their motivation, which is to wake our minds from ignorance. They do not bring their information through the lens of fear, and at the same time, they want us to grow up and catch a clue as to how things are being run on the planet so we can take the steps necessary to take back our power.

There is a definite frequency or feeling that accompanies the arrival of these beings I bring through. Their message is one of empowerment and self-love, and they've explained that they are here to assist as we move through these changing times. They've made it clear that they are not here to be our authority. The fact is that we as human beings require no governing. Guidance by wisdom keepers, yes, but the authorities our culture looks to, carry no wisdom. They are often holding back the truth and have their own game going.

These wise beings like to play with words, saying that language is full of spells, which keeps us anchored to the lower frequencies. When we can recognize how our language traps us in powerlessness, we can shift dramatically. They are very emphatic about the fact that we create with our thoughts. Words carry frequencies, and when we formulate our words without consciousness, we keep ourselves in the same old patterns. Language can be a trap if we don't understand how to work with it. They are emphatic that we learn how to think properly. This means learning how to be critical thinkers rather than trusting an outside authority to tell us how it is. They also discuss numbers and stress the importance of understanding the ancient subjects of sacred geometry, numbers, and astronomy.

White Owl came through me during one channeled session and said that we are, all of us, willing players in a vast holographic game. She said we are "light embodied and so, *Play Light!*" I thought about that. What does light do? Light reveals truth. Light illuminates darkness. As one who chooses to play light, I am inclined to probe deeply into the various subjects I explore. I am a voracious researcher and I am seeing that my "playing light" involves disseminating information and bringing it through so others can see what they may not have noticed before.

The beings recently revealed themselves to me as "Bird Tribe." When I reread my yearlong accounts of my medicine journeys, I realized that this past year of focused, intentioned medicine journeys has been a training of sorts. Through the use of the mushrooms, I had cleared the channels to spirit in such a way that I had become what the ancients recognized as a "medicine oracle." The oracle was mostly the domain of women, who are naturally more intuitive and available. These oracles of old often worked with psychotropic substances to bring them to an altered state where they could connect with extra-dimensional beings. They would then bring through guidance for their community. Examples are the Pythia at Delphi, the Volva in the Norse traditions, and the seers, witches, and shamans from cultures all over the world. They were respected and honored and they lived a life that was dedicated in service to their people.

Recently, I was organizing the many notes I have taken from various classes over the years. I found my notes from a shamanic journey I took to the beat of a drum a couple of years ago. In that journey I found myself standing in front of the Egyptian goddess, Sekhmet. When I read my notes from that journey I felt a full body chill. In that experience Sekhmet said to me, "You are reclaiming the dignity and honor of that which has been cast out. You are cutting a swath through a forest of ignorance, clearing a path for those to come after you to do this work. Teach as many as you can."

I knew it was no accident to have found that writing again. I feel that this is precisely what I am doing through my teaching and writing. I am helping to reclaim old wisdom practices that were once understood and respected. In terms of the use of psychotropic substances, religious organizations and governments have implemented propaganda to demonize the plant medicines for a very long time. I cannot help but feel that there is a deliberate intent to keep us away from these potent expanders of consciousness. The key with entheogens is to use them with reverence, respect, and clear intention, not as a means of escape. There is much to learn from these medicines.

I finish this book with a channeled message from these wise beings that I have connected with. I feel this carries a sound message for these times.

You are beauty dancing, dear ones. Engaged in a cosmic dance of discovery. The discovery of the truth of who you are—flowing, dynamic, loving beings of infinite light and possibility. "Well," you say, "Nothing I haven't already heard." And we ask you dear ones, nothing you haven't already heard, but have you felt it? Have you truly felt yourselves as beauty beings of infinite light and possibility? Do you KNOW yourselves as that? We venture to guess, no.

Too busy, yes? Too distracted with so many things to take care of in your lives. Moments here and there, perhaps, but then you must attend to your lives. And you may wonder, why can we not feel this way all the time? You may even argue for your case, stating that you have to be a certain way to run your life effectively. Well, the circumstances of your life have everything and nothing to do with the truth of who you are.

You are creating in every moment. The more you argue for your limitations, your circumstances—the more ingrained they become. We are suggesting that every cell in your body is listening to your every thought—listening and reacting. So too, the energy around you is responding in kind to your every thought. You think in your language and your language is full of codes. So much in a word—hidden meanings, numbers of letters, and so forth. All of these factors carry frequencies. Words carry frequencies as do sound, numbers, intention, imagination, etc.

How does a spell work? It works when one believes in it, yes? And one can be under a spell and not know it. And so we say pay attention to your language. Pay attention to what you say and how you say it. Pay attention to what is said to you as well, and notice your response. So much is hidden right in front of you. When you can catch the deeper meanings of the words you think, hear, and say, it becomes a game of "ahas." Consider the word, imagination. Can you see magi in imagination? Hmmm? And what have so many of you been told? It's just your *imagination. Well, you are, all of you, magicians in a way. And you have been dancing in limitation for quite some time now.*

We are dropping hints for you, dear ones. We want you to open your ears and your eyes and your hearts and begin to play with those words that compose the thoughts and ideas that you think throughout the day. This is why we want you to catch yourselves when you go into negative thinking, what we call, programs. We say "programs" in a singsong way that sounds like a doorbell ringing—"ding-dong." That is how the word "program" sounds. So, catch your negative thinking with the knowing that it is not the truth of who you are. Simply say to yourself, "program"! Then intend to shift your thinking. Rome wasn't built in a day and so this takes a bit of practice, yes?

You create with your thoughts. Heard that before, haven't you? Well, KNOW it! This is not an intellectual exercise and yet here we are talking about the power of the mind. Couple the power of thoughts with your intention, with your imagination, with your feeling. Come from a clear place with all of that and you'll find yourselves creating a very different reality than the one you are so familiar with. Don't get caught in the trap that things are a certain way and so therefore, cannot be another. That is a limited thought and couldn't be further from the truth.

Everywhere you turn, your external influences are vying for your attention—your media, your governments, and all the other self-described institutions that you give so much credence. Begin to extricate yourself from those outside influences and learn to trust what comes through you. Catch those negative programs when they come, and they come often, don't they? Catch them and clear them, and bring forth a different thought, a different idea. Then cultivate THAT! Give credence to THAT! Believe THAT! You are now in a time where you can access concepts and knowledge that you didn't think were possible. This does not come from your usual sources of information, dear ones. This comes from within you. We are assisting you in clearing the channels as it were, so that your reception is crystal clear!

Have some fun exploring the deeper meanings of the words you say. Do some of your own research on the origins of different words. You may be very surprised at what you discover. This will give new meaning to the phrase, "Choose your words wisely." You are beings of infinite light, love, and possibility. Take charge of yourselves now, dear ones, and look into the power of words. Just as they can be used against you in ways you are not aware of, so too can you use them to create a world of beauty and joy. And don't take our word for it! (Playing here with puns and winking at you.) Do your own experimentation and research and PLAY, dear ones! Discover your power and play with clear intention and love.

From our hearts to yours,

Bird Tribe

Recommended Reading

MUSHROOMS

Allegro, John A. *The Sacred Mushroom and the Cross*. Garden City, NY: Gnostic Media, 2009.

Arthur, James. *Mushrooms and Mankind: The Impact of Mushrooms on Human Consciousness and Religion*. San Diego, CA: The Book Tree, 2000.

Dobkin de Rios, Marlene. *The Psychedelic Journey of Marlene Dobkin de Rios: 45 Years with Shamans, Ayahuasqueros, and Ethnobotanists*. Rochester, VT: Park Street Press, 2009.

Fadiman, James. *The Psychedelic Explorer's Guide*. Rochester, VT: Park Street Press, 2011.

Furst, Peter T. *Flesh of the Gods: The Ritual Use of Hallucinogens*. Prospect Heights, IL: Waveland Press, 1990.

Goldsmith, Neal M. *Psychedelic Healing: The Promise of Entheogens for Psychotherapy and Spiritual Development*. Rochester, VT: Healing Arts Press, 2010.

Hancock, Graham. *Supernatural: Meetings with the Ancient Teachers of Mankind*. New York, NY: The Disinformation Company, 2007.

Harner, Michael J., ed. *Hallucinogens and Shamanism*. New York, NY: Oxford University Press, 1973.

Heinrich, Clark. *Magic Mushrooms in Religion and Alchemy*. Rochester, VT: Park Street Press, 2002.

235

Irvin, Jan. *The Holy Mushroom*. Garden City, NY: Gnostic Media, 2009.

Irvin, Jan, and Andrew Rutajit. *Astrotheology and Shamanism*. Garden City, NY: Gnostic Media, 2009.

McKenna, Terence. *Food of the Gods*. New York, NY: Bantam Books, 1992.

Narby, Jeremy. *The Cosmic Serpent: DNA and the Origins of Knowledge*. New York, NY: Jeremy P. Tarcher/Putnam, 1999.

Nicholas, L.G., and Kerry Ogame. *Psilocybin Mushroom Handbook*. Oakland, CA: Quick American Archives, 2006.

Phillips, Jonathan Talat. *The Electric Jesus: The Healing Journey of a Contemporary Gnostic*. Oakland, CA: Evolver Editions, 2001.

Pinchbeck, Daniel. *Breaking Open the Head*. New York, NY: Broadway Books, 2003.

Ratsch, Christian. *The Encyclopedia of Psychoactive Plants: Ethnopharmacology and Its Applications*. Rochester, VT: Park Street Press, 2005.

Roberts, Thomas B. *Psychedelic Horizons*. Exeter, England: Imprint Academics, 2006.

Roberts, Thomas B., ed. *Spiritual Growth with Entheogens: Psychoactive Sacramentals and Human Transformation*. Rochester, VT: Park Street Press, 2012.

Roberts, Thomas B. *The Psychedelic Future of the Mind: How Entheogens Are Enhancing Cognition, Boosting Intelligence, and Raising Values*. Rochester, VT: Park Street Press, 2013.

Ruck, Carl A.P. *Sacred Mushrooms of the Goddess*. Oakland, CA: Ronin Publishing, 2006.

Ruck, Carl A.P., Mark A. Hoffman, and Jose Alfredo Gonzales Celdran. *Mushrooms, Myth & Mithras: The*

Drug Cult That Civilized Europe. San Francisco, CA: City Lights Publishing, 2011.

Ruck, Carl A.P., and Mark A. Hoffman. *The Effluents of Deity: Alchemy and Psychoactive Sacraments in Medieval and Renaissance Art.* Durham, NC: Carolina Academic Press, 2012.

Ruck, Carl A.P., Blaise Daniel Staples, and Clark Heinrich. *The Apples of Apollo: Pagan and Christian Mysteries of the Eucharist.* Durham, NC: Carolina Academic Press, 2000.

Rush, John A. *The Mushroom in Christian Art: The Identity of Jesus in the Development of Christianity.* Berkeley, CA: North Atlantic Books, 2011.

Schultes, Richard Evans, Albert Hoffman, and Christian Ratsch. *Plants of the Gods: Their Sacred, Healing, and Hallucinogenic Powers.* Rochester, VT: Healing Arts Press, 2001.

Stamets, Paul. *Psilocybin Mushrooms of the World.* Berkeley, CA: Ten Speed Press, 1996.

Stamets, Paul. *Mycelium Running: How Mushrooms Can Help Save the World.* Berkeley, CA: Ten Speed Press, 2005.

Wasson, Gordon, Albert Hoffman, and Carl A.P. Ruck. *The Road to Eleusis: Unveiling the Secret of the Mysteries.* Berkeley, CA: North Atlantic Books, 2008.

RELATIONSHIP

Hendrix, Harville. *Getting the Love You Want: A Guide for Couples.* New York, NY: Henry Holt and Co., 2007.

Hollis, James. *The Middle Passage: From Misery to Meaning in Midlife.* Toronto, Canada: Inner City Books, 1993.

Jung, Emma. *Anima and Animus*. New York, NY: Spring
Publications, 1985.

Sanford, John A. *The Invisible Partners*. Mahwah, NJ: Pau-
list Press, 1979.

Permissions

Archaic Revival Copyright © 1991 by Terrence McKenna
HarperOne, A trademark of HarperCollins Publishers

Psychology and Religion by Carl Jung
Yale University Press; Reprint Edition, September 10th
1960

Aion: Researches into the Phenomenology of the Self (Collected works of C.G. Jung, Volume 9, Part 2)
Princeton University Press, Edition 1, June 1979

Mysterium Conjunctionis by Carl Jung
Princeton University Press, 2nd Edition, (August 1, 1977)

The Road to Eleusis by Carl A.P. Ruck, R. Gordon Wasson
& Albert Hofmann
Copyright © 2008, North Atlantic Books

Split: A Memoir of Divorce
Copyright © 2008 by Suzanne Finnamore. Used by
permission of Dutton, a division of the Penguin Group
(USA) Inc.

Hallucinogens and Shamanism edited by Harner (1973)
166w from pp. 89,95
By permission of Oxford University Press, USA

About the Author

Author, shaman, teacher and oracle, Shonagh Home works with individuals and groups to foster new paradigms and awaken all to their divine nature. Through her training and initiations with master teachers and shamans, she offers a variety of healing modalities and highly transformative classes. She is the author of *Ix Chel Wisdom: 7 Teachings from the Mayan Sacred Feminine*. She teaches in the Pacific Northwest and the Yucatan. Visit her at *www.shonaghhome.com*

Made in the USA
Columbia, SC
04 July 2018